— The Unofficial Guide to
DISNEYLAND® —

The Unofficial Guide to
Disneyland®

New and Revised Edition

Bob Sehlinger

PRENTICE HALL PRESS
NEW YORK

Copyright © 1985, 1987 by Robert W. Sehlinger

All rights reserved including the right of
reproduction in whole or in part in any form

Produced by Menasha Ridge Press

Published by Prentice Hall Press
  A Division of Simon & Schuster, Inc.
  Gulf + Western Building
  One Gulf + Western Plaza
  New York, New York 10023

PRENTICE HALL PRESS is a trademark of
Simon & Schuster, Inc.

Manufactured in the United States of America

Library of Congress Cataloging in Publication Data
Sehlinger, Bob, 1945–
  The unofficial guide to Disneyland

  Includes index.
  1. Disneyland (Calif.)—Guide books. I. Title.
GV1853.3.C22D577 1985   791′.06′879496   86-30599
ISBN: 0-13-937658-5

10 9 8 7 6 5 4 3 2

ISBN: 0-13-937658-5

—— Declaration of Independence ——

The authors and researchers of this guide specifically and categorically declare that they are and always have been totally independent of Walt Disney Productions, Inc., of Disneyland, Inc., of Walt Disney World, Inc., and of any and all other members of the Disney corporate family not listed.

The material in this guide originated with the authors and researchers and has not been reviewed, edited, or in any way approved by Walt Disney Productions, Inc., Disneyland, Inc., or Walt Disney World, Inc.

Contents

List of Illustrations

── *Acknowledgments* ──

Special thanks to our field research team who rendered a Herculean effort in what must have seemed like a fantasy version of Sartre's *No Exit* to the tune of *It's a Small World*. We hope you all recover to tour another day.

Ray Westbrook
Joan W. Burns
Cyril C. Sehlinger
Pid Rafter
Karin Zachow
Paula Owens
Mary Mitchell

Many thanks also to Barbara Williams and Teresa Smith for their design and production of this book. Tseng Information Systems earned our appreciation by keeping tight deadlines in providing the typography.

— The Unofficial Guide to
DISNEYLAND —

How Come "Unofficial"?

This Guidebook represents the first comprehensive critical appraisal of Disneyland. Its purpose is to provide the reader with the information necessary to tour the theme park with the greatest efficiency and economy and with the least amount of hassle and standing in line. The researchers of this guide believe in the wondrous variety, joy, and excitement of the Disney attractions. At the same time we recognize realistically that Disneyland is a business, with the same profit motivations as businesses the world over.

Just as it is impossible for an attorney to represent both sides in the same case, so, too, do we believe that it is impossible in an "official guide" to serve both Disneyland and the consumer. Disneyland naturally wants you to eat in its restaurants, shop in its stores, and tour its attractions. An "official guide" should be a sourcebook of information designed to enhance the appeal of the Disney offering. Tips that would shorten your visit or criticisms (no matter how well founded) that might guide you away from Disney rides, eateries, and shops would have no place in an "official guide."

In this, the "unofficial" guide, we have elected to represent and serve you, the consumer. The contents were researched and compiled by a team of evaluators who were, and are, completely independent of Disneyland and Walt Disney Productions, Inc. If a restaurant serves bad food, or if a gift item is overpriced, or if a certain ride isn't worth the wait, we can say so; in the process, we hope we can make your visit more fun, efficient, and economical.

How This Guide Was Researched and Written

While much has been written concerning Disneyland, very little has been comparative or evaluative. Indeed, most guides simply parrot Disneyland's own promotional material. In preparing this guide, nothing was taken for granted. The theme park was visited at different times throughout the year by a team of trained observers who conducted detailed evaluations, rating the theme park along with all of its component rides, shows, exhibits, services, and concessions according to a formal pretested rating instrument. Interviews with attraction patrons were conducted to determine what tourists of all age groups enjoyed most and least during their Disneyland visit.

While our observers were independent and impartial, we do not claim special expertise or scientific background relative to the types of exhibits, performances, or attractions viewed. Like you, we visit Disneyland as tourists, noting our satisfaction or dissatisfaction. Disney offerings are marketed to the touring public, and it is as the public that we have experienced them.

The primary difference between the average tourist and the trained evaluator is in the evaluator's professional skills in organization, preparation, and observation. The trained evaluator is responsible for much more than simply observing and cataloging. While the tourist seated next to him is being entertained and delighted at the Enchanted Tiki Room, the professional is rating the performance in terms of theme, pace, continuity, and originality. He is also checking out the physical arrangements: is the sound system clear and audible without being overpowering; is the audience shielded from the sun or rain; is seating adequate; can everyone in the audience clearly see the staging area? And what about guides and/or performers: are they knowledgeable, articulate, and professional in their presentation; are they friendly and engaging? Does the performance begin and end on time; does the show contain the features described in Disneyland's promotional literature? These and many other considerations figure prominently in the rating of any staged performance. Similarly, detailed and relevant checklists were prepared and applied by observer teams to rides, exhibits, concessions, and to the theme park in general. Finally observations and evaluator ratings were integrated with audience reactions and the opinions of patrons to compile a comprehensive quality profile of each feature and service.

In compiling this guide, we recognize the fact that a tourist's age, sex, background, and interests will strongly influence his taste in Disneyland offerings and will account for his/her preference of one ride or feature over another. Given this fact, we make no attempt at comparing apples with oranges. How indeed could a meaningful comparison be made between the serenity and beauty of the Storybook Land Canal Boats and the wild roller coaster ride of Space Mountain. Instead, our objective is to provide the reader with a critical evaluation and enough pertinent data to make knowledgeable decisions according to his individual tastes.

The essence of this guide, then, consists of individual critiques and descriptions of each feature of Disneyland, supplemented with some maps to help you get around and several detailed Touring Plans to help you avoid bottlenecks and crowds.

Disneyland — An Overview

If you are selecting among the tourist attractions of California, the question is not whether to visit Disneyland but how to see the best of the various Disney offerings with some economy of time, effort, and finances.

Make no mistake: there is nothing quite like Disneyland. Incredible in its scope, genius, beauty, and imagination, it is a joy and wonderment for people of all ages. A fantasy, a dream, and a vision all rolled into one, it transcends simple entertainment, making us children and adventurers, freeing us for an hour or a day to live the dreams of our past, present, and future.

Disneyland, even more than its Florida counterpart, embodies that quiet, charming spirit of nostalgia which so characterized Walt Disney himself. Disneyland is vast yet intimate, etched in the tradition of its founder, yet continually changing. A visit to Disneyland is fun, but it is also a powerful and moving experience, a living testimony to the achievements and immense potential of the loving and life-embracing side of man's creativity.

Certainly we are critics, but it is the responsibility of critics to credit that which is done well as surely as to reflect negatively on that which is done poorly. The Disney attractions are special, a quantum leap beyond and above any man-made entertainment offering we know of. It is incredible to us that anyone could visit southern California and bypass Disneyland.

—— What Does Disneyland Consist Of? ——

Disneyland was opened in 1955 on a 107-acre tract surrounded almost exclusively by vegetable farms just west of the sleepy, and little known, southern California community of Anaheim. Constrained by finances and ultimately enveloped by the city it helped to create, Disneyland operates still on that same modest parcel of land. On what amounts to a huge city block resides the Disneyland Theme Park, its backlot and service area, and its ample visitor parking lot.

The theme park is a collection of adventures, rides, and shows symbolized by the Disney cartoon characters and the Sleeping Beauty Castle. Disneyland is divided into seven sub-areas or "lands" arranged around a central hub. First encountered is Main Street USA which connects the Disneyland entrance with the central hub. Moving clockwise around the hub, the other lands are Adventureland, Frontierland, Fantasyland, and Tomorrowland. The two remaining major lands, Bear Country and New Orleans Square, are accessible via Adventureland and Frontierland but do not connect directly with the central hub. All seven lands will be described in detail later.

Located across West Street and connected to the theme park by the Disneyland Monorail system is the Disneyland Hotel, operated as a concession by the Wrather Hotel chain. Unlike the Florida Disney development, there are no subsidiary theme parks, golf courses, campgrounds, or other associated projects.

Some visitors expect to be able to tour the Walt Disney Productions studio while at Disneyland. The studio, alas, is some miles distant, in Burbank, California, and does not offer tours.

— *Growth and Change at Disneyland* —

Growth and change at Disneyland have been internal in marked contrast to the ever enlarging development of spacious Walt Disney World near Orlando, Florida. When something new is added at Disneyland, something old must go. The Disney engineers, to their credit, however, have never been shy about disturbing the status quo. Patrons of the park's earlier, more modest years are amazed by the transformation. Gone are the days of the "magical little park" with the Monsanto House of the Future, flying saucer style bumper cars, and Captain Hook's Pirate Ship. Substituted in a process of continuous evolution and modernization are "state of the art" fourth and fifth generation attractions and entertainments. To paraphrase Walt Disney, Disneyland will never stop changing as long as there are new ideas to explore.

Disneyland, like any business, is subject to trends. The current trend translates into a rather sustained effort to improve the park's appeal to the local population and to teens. The attempt to appeal to teenagers signifies a new direction for Disneyland. Under Walt Disney's leadership the attraction focused on entertainment "for the whole family"— in part, a euphemism for "Walt don't want no rock 'n' roll round here." Today, however, in Walt's absence, there is lots of rock 'n' roll at Disneyland. In addition to developing its own rock groups which play regularly on the Tomorrowland Terrace stage, and to guest concerts by the country's hottest rock bands, Disneyland has installed a major theater showing a Michael Jackson rock movie which will run continuously. And that ain't all. A multimillion-dollar complex adjacent to Small World in Fantasyland features live rock, rock videos, and dancing.

— *Should I Go to Disneyland If I've Seen Walt Disney World?* —

Disneyland is roughly comparable to the Magic Kingdom theme park at Walt Disney World near Orlando, Florida. Both are arranged by "lands" accessible from a central hub and connected to the entrance by a Main Street. Both parks feature many rides and attractions of the same name: Space Mountain, Jungle Cruise, Pirates of the Caribbean, It's a Small World, and Dumbo the Flying Elephant, to name a few. Interestingly, however, the same name does not necessarily connote the same experience. Pirates of the Caribbean at Disneyland is much longer and more elaborate than its Walt Disney World counterpart. Space Mountain is far wilder in Florida, and Dumbo is about the same in both places.

Disneyland is more intimate than the Magic Kingdom, not having the room for expansion enjoyed by the Florida park. Pedestrian thoroughfares are narrower, and everything from Big Thunder Mountain to the Castle is scaled down somewhat. Large crowds are more taxing at Disneyland since there is less room for them to disperse. At Disneyland, however, there are dozens of little surprises, small unheralded attractions tucked away in crooks and corners of the park, which give Disneyland a special charm and variety that the Magic Kingdom lacks. And, of course, Disneyland has the stamp of Walt Disney's personal touch.

To allow for a meaningful comparison, we provide a summary of those features found only at Disneyland followed by a critical look at the attractions found at both parks.

Attractions Found Only at Disneyland

Main Street:	*Great Moments with Mr. Lincoln*
Frontierland:	Sailing Ship Columbia
	Big Thunder Ranch

Fantasyland:	The Story of Sleeping Beauty
	Pinocchio's Daring Journey
	Casey Jr. Circus Train
	Storybook Land Canal Boats
	Alice in Wonderland
	Matterhorn Bobsleds
	Motor Boat Cruise
	Videopolis
Tomorrowland:	*America Sings*
	Star Tours

Critical Comparison of Attractions Found at Both Parks

Main Street

WDW/Disneyland Railroad	The Disneyland Railroad is far more entertaining by virtue of the Grand Canyon Diorama and the Primeval World components not found at the Magic Kingdom.
The Walt Disney Story	More comprehensive film at the Magic Kingdom. More interesting static displays and memorabilia at Disneyland.

Adventureland

Jungle Cruise	More realistic AudioAnimatronic (robotic) animals at Walt Disney World, otherwise about the same.
Enchanted Tiki Room	About the same at both parks.
Swiss Family Treehouse	Larger at the Magic Kingdom.

New Orleans Square

Pirates of the Caribbean	Far superior at Disneyland.
Haunted Mansion	Slight edge to the Magic Kingdom version.

Bear Country

Country Bear Jamboree	Same production with a much shorter wait at Disneyland.

Frontierland

Various river cruises (Canoes, boats, etc.)	More interesting sights at the Magic Kingdom.

Tom Sawyer Island	Comparable, but a little more elaborate with better food service at the Magic Kingdom.
Big Thunder Mountain Railroad	Ride about the same. Sights and special effects are better at the Magic Kingdom.
Golden Horseshoe Revue/Diamond Horseshoe Revue	Similar at both parks.

Fantasyland

Snow White's Scary Adventures	About the same at both parks.
Peter Pan's Flight	Better at Disneyland.
Mr. Toad's Wild Ride	Better at Disneyland.
Dumbo the Flying Elephant	The same at both parks.
Carousels	About the same at both parks.
Castles	Far larger and more beautiful at the Magic Kingdom.
Mad Tea Party	The same at both parks.
It's a Small World	About the same at both parks.
Skyway	About the same at both parks.

Tomorrowland

Autopia/Grand Prix Raceway	About the same at both parks.
Mission to Mars	The same at both parks.
Rocket Jets/Starjets	The same at both parks.
PeopleMover	The edge goes to Disneyland.
World Premier Circle-Vision	The same at both parks.
Space Mountain	Vastly superior in terms of both ride and special effects at the Magic Kingdom.
Submarine Voyage/ 20,000 Leagues	About the same at both parks.

PART ONE—Planning Before You Leave Home

— Gathering Information —

In addition to this guide, information concerning Disneyland can be obtained at the public library, through travel agencies, or by writing or calling:

Disneyland Guest Relations
P. O. Box 3232
Anaheim, California 92803
telephone (714) 999-4565

— Admission Options —

One day, two day, and three day admission passes are available for purchase for both adults (13 years and up) and children (3 to 12 years inclusive). All rides, shows, and attractions (except the Frontierland Shooting Arcade) are included in the price of admission. Multi-day passes do not have to be used on consecutive days.

Admission prices, not unexpectedly, are increased from time to time. To plan your budget, however, you can assume that a one-day pass for an adult will cost about four times the price of a first-run movie. Two-day passes will cost around seven times the price of a first-run movie with three-day passes costing in the neighborhood of nine times the expense of a first-run film. Children's admissions run roughly two-thirds the cost of an adult admission.

Timing Your Visit

— Selecting the Time of Year for Your Visit —

Crowds are largest at Disneyland during the summer (Memorial Day to Labor Day) and during specific holiday periods during the rest of the year. The busiest time of all is Christmas Day through New Year's Day. Thanksgiving weekend, the week of Washington's Birthday, spring break for colleges, and the two weeks around Easter are also extremely busy. To give you some idea of what busy means at Disneyland, more than 77,000 people have toured the park on a single day! While this level of attendance is far from typical, the possibility of its occurrence should prevent all but the ignorant and the foolish from challenging this mega-attraction at its busiest periods.

The least busy time of all is from after the Thanksgiving Weekend until the week before Christmas. The next slowest times are September through the weekend preceding Thanksgiving, January 4th through the first half of March, and the week following Easter to Memorial Day. At the risk of being blasphemous, our research team was so impressed with the relative ease of touring in the fall and other "off" periods that we would rather take our children out of school for a few days than to do battle with the summer crowds.

— Selecting the Day of the Week for Your Visit —

The crowds at Walt Disney World in Florida are comprised of mostly out-of-state visitors. Not necessarily so at Disneyland, which, along with Knott's Berry Farm, serves as an often-frequented recreational resource to the greater Los Angeles and San Diego communities. To many Southern Californians, Disneyland is less of a tourist attraction than it is their private theme park. Yearly passes are available at less cost than a year's membership to the YMCA, and the Disney management has intensified its efforts to appeal to the local market.

What all this means is that weekends are usually packed. Saturday is

Visitors per Day (thousands)

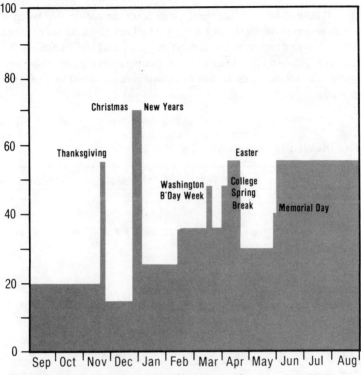

(Attendance figures represent weekly averages)

the busiest day of the entire week. Sunday is the best bet if you have to go on a weekend, but is nevertheless extremely busy. Sunday *mornings*, however, are often slow and afford relatively crowd-free touring opportunities for those who arrive when the park opens. Sunday evenings, likewise, are comparatively slow.

During the summer, Monday and Tuesday are very busy, Wednesday and Thursday usually less so, and Friday is normally the slowest day of all. During the "off season" (September–May, holiday periods excepted) Friday remains the least crowded day, usually followed by Thursday, with Monday, Tuesday, and Wednesday varying somewhat. Disneyland is sometimes closed on Monday and Tuesday from October through February.

—— Operating Hours ——

It cannot be said that the Disney folks are not flexible when it comes to hours of operation for the park. They run a dozen or more different operating schedules during the year, making it advisable to call (714) 999-4565 for the **exact** hours of operation the day before you arrive. The following table, however, will give a general idea of what to expect.

Regular (Non-Holiday) Hours*

	Weekdays	Saturday	Sunday
Winter (December–February)	10 A.M.–6 P.M.	10 A.M.–7 P.M.	10 A.M.–7 P.M.
Spring (March–May)	10 A.M.–6 P.M.	9 A.M.–9 P.M.	9 A.M.–9 P.M.
Summer (June)	9 A.M.–9 P.M.	9 A.M.–midnight	9 A.M.–9 P.M.
Summer (July–August)	9 A.M.–midnight	9 A.M.–1 A.M.	9 A.M.–midnight
Fall (September–November)	10 A.M.–6 P.M.	9 A.M.–9 P.M.	9 A.M.–9 P.M.

* Hours given represent the norm. For specific hours of operation call (714) 999-4565 in advance of your visit. Hours for most major holidays are 9 A.M.–midnight, but once again it is advisable to call for specifics.

—— Official Opening Time vs. Real Opening Time ——

The hours of operation listed above, as well as the hours the Disneyland folks will give you when you call, are "official hours." In actuality the park will open earlier. If the official hours of operation are 9 A.M.–9 P.M., for example, the Main Street section of Disneyland will open at 8 A.M. and the remainder of the park will open at 8:30 A.M. Many visitors, assuming the accuracy of the information disseminated by the Disney Guest Relations service, arrive at the stated opening time to find the park fairly thronged with people.

Usually you can depend on Main Street opening an hour in advance of the stated official opening time, with the rest of Disneyland opening half an hour before the official opening time. We recommend arriving an hour before the official opening time regardless of the time of year of your visit. If you happen to go on a major holiday, arrive an hour and twenty minutes in advance of the official opening time.

As concerns closing time, the Disney people usually close everything but Main Street at approximately the official stated closing time. Main Street remains open a half hour to an hour after the rest of the park has closed.

— *Packed Park Compensation Plan* —

The thought of teeming, jostling throngs jockeying for position in endless lines under the baking Fourth of July sun is enough to wilt the will and ears of the most ardent Mouseketeer. Why would anyone go to Disneyland on a summer Saturday or during a major holiday period? Indeed, if you have never been to Disneyland, and you thought you would just drop in for a few rides and a little look-see on such a day, you might be better off shooting yourself in the foot. The Disney folks, however, being Disney folks, feel kind of bad about those long, long lines and the basically impossible touring conditions on packed days and compensate their patrons with a no less than incredible array of first-rate live entertainment and happenings.

Throughout the day the party goes on with shows, parades, concerts, and pageantry. In the evening there is so much going on that you have to make some tough choices. Big-name music groups perform on the River Stage in Frontierland and at the Videopolis in Fantasyland. Other concerts are produced concurrently at the Golden Horseshoe and in Tomorrowland. There are always parades, sometimes fireworks, and the Disney characters make frequent appearances. Stage shows and rock concerts are presented at the Plaza Gardens (off the central hub) and at Tomorrowland Terrace. No question about it, you can go to Disneyland on the Fourth of July (or any other extended-hours, crowded day), never get on a ride, and still get your money's worth five times over. Admittedly, it's not the ideal situation for a first-timer who really wants to see the park, but for anyone else it's one heck of a good party.

If you decide to go on one of the park's "big" days, we suggest that you arrive an hour and twenty minutes before the stated opening time. Use the Disneyland One-Day Touring Plan of your choice until about 1 P.M. and then take the Monorail to the Disneyland Hotel for lunch and relaxation. Southern Californian visitors often chip in and rent a room for the group (make reservations well in advance) in the Disneyland Hotel, thus affording a place to meet, relax, have a drink, or change clothes prior to enjoying the pools at the Hotel. A comparable arrangement can be made at other nearby hotels as long as they furnish a shuttle service to and from the park. After an early dinner return to the park for the evening's festivities which really get cranked up about 8 P.M.

Getting There

At Walt Disney World in Florida, automobile traffic enters and exits via four-lane expressways which connect directly to interstate highways. At Disneyland, unfortunately, automobile access is not so streamlined. To begin with, Disneyland is close to, but not directly connected to, Interstate 5 (Santa Ana Freeway). Exit signs on the freeway give the impression that one exit provides as easy an access to Disneyland as the next. In fact, only the Harbor Boulevard exit allows direct access to the park without multiple turns and traffic signals.

The freeways themselves are capricious in the extreme, with congestion and bumper-to-bumper traffic likely to erupt at almost any hour of the day. Add to this prevailing confusion the crunch of rush-hour traffic, and you have the best reason imaginable for choosing a hotel as close to Disneyland as possible. Our research team lodged in Laguna Beach and commuted to the park each day. Driving the same distance on every trip, our transportation time to the park ranged from 25 minutes to $2\frac{1}{2}$ hours. Disney employees have devised complex routings through subdivisions and city streets in order to beat the freeway mess and be at work on time.

When the park opens early or closes early, Anaheim rush-hour traffic and Disneyland rush-hour traffic literally meet head on, tying up the streets and freeways surrounding the park for miles. Early (6 P.M.) closings create the greatest confusion with an en masse departure of park patrons attempting to fight their way out of the parking lot and onto city streets and freeways jammed with local commuters.

And don't expect the same Disney efficiency in emptying the parking lot as in filling it. There will be lots of Disney employees to help you park in the morning, but virtually none to help you get out in the evening.

To make the most of an almost intolerable traffic situation we make the following recommendations:

1. Stay as close to Disneyland as possible.

2. If you stay some distance from Disneyland (five miles or more), leave for the park extra early, say an hour or more. If you get lucky and don't encounter too many problems you can relax over breakfast at a restaurant near Disneyland while you wait for the park to open.

3. If you must use the Santa Ana Freeway, give yourself lots of extra time, and exit onto Harbor Boulevard. This will feed you directly into the Disneyland lot with no left turns.

4. If you must use the Garden Grove Freeway, exit onto Euclid Street, turn right onto Ball Road, and finally right onto Harbor Boulevard. This will take you into the Disneyland lot without any left turns.

5. Try to avoid Disneyland on days when the park closes at 6 P.M. If your schedule allows no alternative, either leave before 4:30 (you will be able to get out of the parking lot, but will almost certainly get stuck in the local rush-hour traffic) or stay in the park until Main Street closes (half an hour after the rest of the park) and steel yourself for some major-league problems getting out of the parking lot.

—— *Taking a Tram or Shuttle Bus from Your Hotel* ——

Trams and shuttle buses are provided by many hotels and motels in the vicinity of Disneyland. They represent a fairly carefree alternative for getting to and from the theme park, letting you off right at the entrance and saving you the cost of parking. The rub is that they might not get you there as early as you desire (a critical point if you take our touring advice) or be available at the time you wish to return to your lodging. Also, some shuttles are direct to Disneyland while others make stops at other motels and hotels in the vicinity. Each shuttle service is a little bit different so check out the particulars when you arrive at your hotel. If the shuttle provided by your hotel runs regularly throughout the day to and from Disneyland, and if you have the flexibility to tour the park over two or three days, the shuttle provides a wonderful opportunity to tour in the morning and return to your lodging for lunch, a swim, or perhaps a nap, heading back to Disneyland refreshed in the early evening for a little more fun.

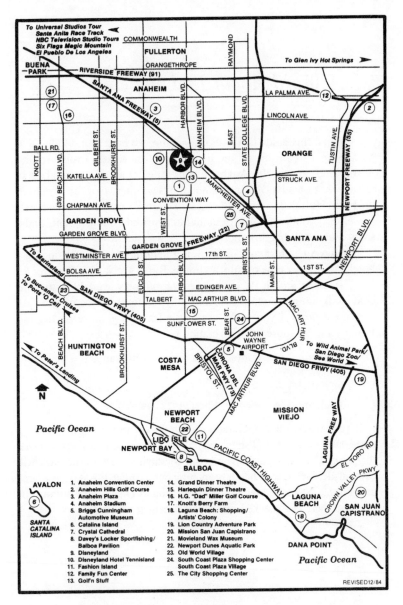

Map 1. Anaheim and surrounding areas

Source: Anaheim/Orange County Travel Agent Guide, 1985/86. Reproduced courtesy of the Anaheim Visitor & Convention Bureau.

A Word About Lodging

While this guide is not about lodging, we have found lodging to be a primary concern of those visiting Disneyland. Traffic around Disneyland, and in the Anaheim–Los Angeles area in general, is so terrible that we advocate accommodations within two or three miles of the park. Included in this radius are, of course, many expensive hotels as well as a goodly number of moderately priced establishments and a small number of bargain motels.

The AAA California Tour Book is a helpful reference for finding a hotel. Another source of information is Rand McNally's *Lodging for Less, Western States*. Package tours are routinely available which include lodging, park admission, and other features. Some of these are very good deals if you make use of the features you are paying for. Finally, a good source of information is:

Anaheim Area Visitor and Convention Bureau
800 W. Katella
P.O. Box 4270
Anaheim, CA 92803   Phone (714) 999-8999

If your travel plans include a stay in the area of more than two or three days, lodge near Disneyland only before and on the days you visit the park. The same traffic you avoid by staying close to the park will eat you alive when you begin branching out to other Los Angeles–area attractions. Also, the area immediately around Disneyland is uninspiring, and there is a marked scarcity of decent restaurants.

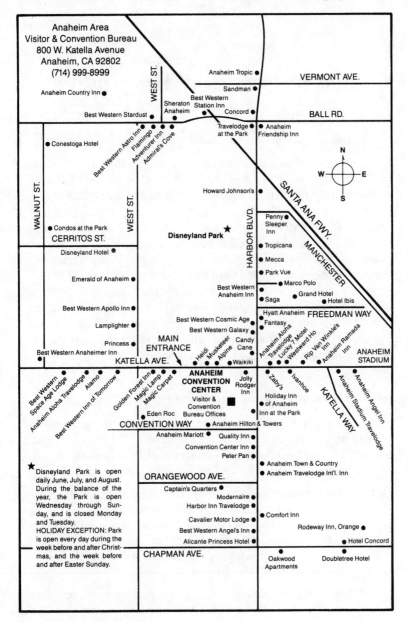

Map 2. Lodging in the Anaheim area

Source: Anaheim/Orange County Travel Agent Guide, 1985/86. Reproduced courtesy of the Anaheim Visitor & Convention Bureau.

Making the Most of Your Time

Allocating Time

The Disney people recommend a day and a half to three full days at Disneyland. While this may seem a little self-serving, it is not without basis. Disneyland is HUGE, with something to see or do crammed into every conceivable space. In addition, touring requires a lot of walking and often a lot of waiting in lines. Moving in and among large crowds all day is exhausting, and oftentimes the unrelenting southern California sun zaps the most hardy, making tempers short. In our many visits to Disneyland we observed, particularly on hot summer days, a dramatic transition from happy, enthusiastic touring upon arrival to an almost zombie-like plodding along later in the day. Visitors who began their day enjoying the wonders of Disney imagination ultimately lapsed into an exhausted production mentality ("We've got two more rides in Fantasyland, then we can go back to the hotel").

—— Optimum Touring Situation ——

The optimum touring situation would call for having three days of touring time at your disposal. Buy the Three-Day Passport which entitles you to admission plus unlimited use of attractions and experiences; it does not have to be used on consecutive days.

Day One:
Tour Disneyland early in the morning when the lines are short and the day is cooler, following Day One of the Two-Day Touring Plan provided in this guide to help you avoid long lines. At about noon go back to your hotel for lunch and maybe a swim or a nap—whatever you feel like.

If the park closes early (6 to 8 P.M.), return refreshed about two hours before closing and continue your visit in the relative cool and diminished crowds of the evening. Eat dinner somewhere outside of Disneyland after the park closes.

If Disneyland closes late (9 P.M. to I A.M.), eat a relaxed dinner outside the park and return refreshed to enjoy yourself until closing time. Evenings on a late closing night are special at Disneyland. We recommend this time for taking in parades and other live performances. If you stay until near closing you will find the lines for the more popular rides vastly diminished.

Day Two: Arrive early in the morning and follow Day Two of the Two-Day Touring Plan provided in this guide.

If the park closes early stick around for the afternoon parade and some of the other live performances around the park. Visit Tom Sawyer Island before dusk. If you enjoy shopping, this is a good time to explore the shops.

If the park remains open late, eat an early dinner outside Disneyland, and return around 7:30 to enjoy the evening festivities.

Day Three: Arrive early and experience again those rides and attractions which you enjoyed most from the first two mornings. Catch any of the shows or rides you missed on the previous days.

The essence of the foregoing "Optimum Touring Situation" is to see the various attractions of Disneyland in a series of shorter, less exhausting visits during the cooler, less crowded parts of the day, with plenty of rest and relaxation in between visits. Since the "Optimum Touring Situation" calls for exiting and returning to Disneyland on most days, it obviously makes for easier logistics if you are staying fairly close to the park (five miles or less to your hotel). If you are lodged too far away for a great deal of coming and going, try relaxing during the heat of the day in the lounges or at the pools of the Disneyland Hotel complex.

—— *Seeing Disneyland on a Tight Schedule* ——

Many visitors do not have three days to devote to Disneyland. Some are en route to other California destinations while others wish to spend time sampling other attractions. For these visitors, efficient, time-effective touring is a must. They cannot afford long waits in line for rides, shows, or meals.

Even the most efficient touring plan will not allow the visitor to cover Disneyland in one day without making some choices. The basic trade-off is between enjoying the rides or catching specially scheduled live entertainment such as parades, concerts, etc. If the park closes late (9 P.M. or later), you can with a little organization have the best of both worlds. If, however, the park closes early, you will probably have to give up seeing some of the attractions.

One-Day Touring

Comprehensively touring Disneyland in one day is possible but requires a knowledge of the park, good planning, and no small reserve of energy and endurance. One-day touring does not leave much time for leisurely meals in sit-down restaurants, prolonged browsing in the many shops, or lengthy rest periods. Even so, one-day touring can be a fun and rewarding experience.

Successful one-day touring hinges on THREE CARDINAL RULES:

1. *Determine in Advance What You Really Want to See*

What are the rides and attractions that appeal to you most? Which additional rides and attractions would you like to experience if you have any time left? What are you willing to forego? The section of this guide labeled "Disneyland in Detail" will help you sort out your choices. Also refer to the section on Live Entertainment.

2. *Arrive Early! Arrive Early! Arrive Early!*

This is the single most important key to efficient touring and avoiding long lines. Have your admission pass and be at the gate ready to go an hour before the theme park's stated opening time. First thing in the morning there are no lines and relatively few people. The same five rides which you can experience in one hour in the early morning will take more than three hours to see after 11:30 A.M. Have breakfast before you arrive so you will not have to waste prime touring time sitting in a restaurant.

3. *Avoid Bottlenecks*

Helping you avoid bottlenecks is what this guide is all about. Bottlenecks occur as a result of crowd concentrations and/or less than optimal traffic engineering. Concentrations of hungry people create bottlenecks at restaurants during the lunch and dinner hours; concentrations of people moving towards the exit near closing time create bottlenecks in the gift shops en route to the gate; concentrations of visitors at new and unusually popular rides create bottlenecks and long waiting lines; rides which are slow in loading and unloading passengers create bottlenecks and long waiting lines. Avoiding bottlenecks involves being able to predict where, when, and why they occur. To this end we provide field-tested **Touring Plans** to keep you ahead of the crowd or out of its way. In addition we provide **Critical Data** on all rides and shows which help you to estimate how long you may have to wait in line, which compare rides in terms of their capacity to accommodate large crowds, and which rate the rides according to our opinions and the opinions of other Disneyland visitors.

—— *Traffic Patterns Inside Disneyland* ——

When we began our research on Disneyland, we were very interested in traffic patterns throughout the park, specifically:

1. *What attractions and which sections of the park do visitors head for when they first arrive?*

When visitors are admitted to the various lands, the flow of people to Tomorrowland, Fantasyland, Adventureland, and New Orleans Square is almost equal. The initial flow to Frontierland and Bear Country is slightly less. In our research we tested the assertion, often heard, that most people turn right into Tomorrowland and tour Disneyland in an orderly counterclockwise fashion, and found it without basis. As the park fills, visitors appear to head for specific favored attractions that they wish to ride before the lines get long. This more than any other factor determines traffic patterns in the mornings and accounts for the relatively equal distribution of visitors throughout Disneyland. Attractions which receive considerable patronage in the early morning are:

Captain EO	Tomorrowland
Star Tours	Tomorrowland
Space Mountain	Tomorrowland
Golden Horseshoe Revue	Frontierland
Big Thunder Mountain Railroad	Frontierland
Matterhorn Bobsleds	Fantasyland
Jungle Cruise	Adventureland
Pirates of the Caribbean	New Orleans Square

2. *How long does it take for the park to reach peak capacity for a given day? How are the visitors dispersed throughout the park?*

There is a surge of "early birds" who arrive before and approximately at opening time but who are quickly absorbed into the empty park. After opening there is a steady stream of arriving visitors which peaks between 10 and 11 A.M.

Lines sampled reach their longest length between 12 noon and 2 P.M., indicating more arrivals than park departures into the early afternoon. For general touring purposes, most attractions develop substantial lines between 10:30 and 11:30 A.M. Through the early hours of the morning and the early hours of the afternoon, attendance is fairly equally distributed through all of the "lands." By mid-afternoon, however, we noted a concentration of visitors in Fantasyland and New Orleans Square and a slight decrease of visitors in Bear Country and in Tomorrowland. This pattern did not occur consistently day to day, but did happen often enough for us to suggest Tomorrowland as the best bet for mid-afternoon touring.

Late afternoon and early evening normally found attendance more heavily distributed in Tomorrowland and Fantasyland than in Adventureland, New Orleans Square, Bear Country, and Frontierland. This trend usually continues and becomes more pronounced as the evening progresses.

3. *How do most visitors go about touring the park? Is there a difference in the touring behavior of first-time visitors and repeat visitors?*

Many first-time visitors accompany friends or relatives who are familiar with Disneyland and who guide their tour. These tours sometimes do and sometimes do not proceed in an orderly (clockwise or counterclockwise) touring sequence. First-time visitors without personal touring guidance tend to be more orderly in their touring. Many first-time visitors, however, are drawn to Sleeping Beauty Castle upon entering the park and thus commence their rotation from Fantasyland. Repeat visitors usually proceed directly to their favorite attractions.

4. *What effect do special events, such as the daily Main Street Parade, have on traffic patterns?*

Special events such as the Main Street Parade do pull substantial numbers of visitors from the ride lines, but the key to the length of the lines remains the number of people in the park.

5. *What are the traffic patterns near to and at closing time?*

On our sample days, recorded in and out of season, park departures outnumbered arrivals beginning in mid-afternoon, with a wave of departures following the parade(s). A substantial number of visitors departed during the late afternoon as the dinner hour approached. When the park closed early, there were steady departures during the two hours preceding closing time, with a mass exodus of remaining visitors at closing time. When the park closed late, departures were distributed throughout the evening hours, with waves of departures following the evening parade(s), increasing as closing time approached. The balloon effect of mass departures at the end of the day primarily affects conditions on Main Street and in the parking complex. In the lands other than Main Street just prior to closing, touring conditions are normally uncrowded.

— *Saving Time in Line* by Understanding the Rides —

There are many different types of rides in Disneyland. Some rides, like It's a Small World, are engineered to carry several thousand people every hour. At the other extreme, rides such as Dumbo the Flying Elephant can only accommodate around 300 persons in an hour. Most rides fall somewhere in between. Lots of factors figure into how long you will have to wait to experience a particular ride: the popularity of the ride, how it loads and unloads, how many persons can ride at one time, how many units (cars, rockets, boats, Flying Elephants, Skyway gondolas, etc.) of those available are in service at a given time, and how many staff personnel are available to operate the ride. Let's take them one by one:

1. *Popularity of the ride.* Newer rides like the Star Tours space flight attract a lot of people, as do longtime favorites such as the Jungle Cruise. If you know a ride is popular, you need to learn a little more about how it operates to determine when might be the best time to ride. But a ride need not be especially popular to form long lines: the lines can be the result of less than desirable traffic engineering; that is, it takes so long to load and unload that a line builds up anyway. This is the situation at the Mad Tea Party and Dumbo the Flying Elephant.

Only a small percentage of the visitors to Disneyland (mostly children) ride Dumbo, for instance, but because it takes so long to load and unload, this comparatively unpopular ride can form long waiting lines.

2. *How the ride loads and unloads.* Some rides never stop. They are like a circular conveyor belt that goes around and around. We call these "continuous loaders." The Haunted Mansion is a continuous loader. The more cars or ships or whatever are on the conveyor, the more people can be moved through in an hour. The Haunted Mansion has lots of cars on the conveyor belt and consequently can move more than 2,400 people an hour.

Other rides are interval loaders. This means that cars are unloaded, loaded, and dispatched at certain set intervals (sometimes controlled manually and sometimes by a computer). Matterhorn Bobsleds is an interval loader. It has two separate tracks (in other words, the ride has been duplicated in the same facility). Each track can run up to 10 sleds, released at 23-second or greater intervals (the bigger the crowd the shorter the interval). In one kind of interval loader, like Space Mountain, empty cars (space capsules) are returned to the starting point, where they line up waiting to be reloaded. In a second type of interval loader, one group of riders enters the vehicle while the last group of riders depart. We call these "in and out" interval loaders. It's a Small World is a good example of an "in and out" interval loader. As a boat pulls up to the dock, those who have just completed their ride exit to the left. At almost the same time, those waiting to ride enter the boat from the right. The boat is released to the dispatch point a few yards down the line where it is launched according to whatever second interval is being used. Interval loaders of both types can be very efficient at moving people if (1) the release (launch) interval is relatively short, and (2) the ride can accommodate a large number of vehicles in the system at one time. Since many boats can be floating through Pirates of the Caribbean at a given time, and since the release interval is short, almost 2,300 people an hour can see this attraction. Submarine Voyage is an "in and out" interval loader, but can only run a maximum of 8 submarines at a time. Thus Submarine Voyage can only handle up to 1,700 people per hour.

A third group of rides are "cycle rides." Another name for these same rides is "stop and go" rides. Here those waiting to ride exchange places with those who have just ridden. The main difference between "in and out" interval rides and cycle rides is that with a cycle ride the whole system shuts down when loading and unloading is in progress. While one boat is loading and unloading in It's a Small World, many other boats are proceeding through the ride. But when Dumbo the Flying Elephant touches down, the whole ride is at a standstill until the next flight is launched. Likewise, with the Rocket Jets, all riders dismount and the Jets stand stationary until the next group is loaded and ready to ride. In discussing a cycle ride, the amount of time the ride is in motion is called "ride time." The amount of time that the ride is idle while loading and unloading is called "load time." Load time plus ride time equals "cycle time," or the time expended from the start of one run of the ride until the start of the succeeding run. Cycle rides are the least efficient of all the Disneyland rides in terms of traffic engineering.

3. *How many persons can ride at one time.* This figure is defined in terms of "per-ride capacity" or "system capacity." Either way, the figures refer to the number of people who can be riding at the same time. Our discussion above illustrates that the greater the carrying capacity of a ride (all other things being equal), the more visitors it can accommodate in an hour.

4. *How many units are in service at a given time.* A "unit" is simply our term for the vehicle you sit in during your ride. At the Mad Tea Party the unit is a Tea Cup, at the Submarine Voyage it's a submarine, and at Alice in Wonderland it's a caterpillar. On some rides (mostly cycle rides), the number of units in operation at a given time is fixed. Thus there are always 10 Flying Elephant units operating on the Dumbo ride, 72 horses on King Arthur Carousel, and so on. What this fixed number of units means to you is that there is no way to increase the carrying capacity of the ride by adding more units. On a busy day, therefore, the only way to carry more people each hour on a fixed-unit cycle ride is to shorten the loading time (which, as we will see in section 5 below, is sometimes impossible) or by decreasing the riding time, the actual time the ride is in motion. The bottom line on a busy day for a cycle ride is that you will wait longer and be rewarded for your wait with a shorter ride. This is why we try to steer you clear of the cycle rides unless you are willing to ride them early in the morning or late at night. The following rides are cycle rides:

Fantasyland:	Dumbo the Flying Elephant
	King Arthur Carousel
	Mad Tea Party
Tomorrowland:	Rocket Jets

Other rides at Disneyland can increase their carrying capacity by adding additional units to the system as the crowds build. Big Thunder Mountain is a good example. If attendance is very light, Big Thunder can start the day by running one of their five available mine trains on one out of two available tracks. If lines start to build, the other track can be opened and more mine trains placed into operation. At full capacity a total of five trains on two tracks can carry about 2,400 persons an hour. Likewise Pirates of the Caribbean can increase its capacity by adding more boats, and Snow White's Scary Adventures by adding more mine cars. Sometimes a long line will disappear almost instantly when new units are brought on line. When an interval loading ride places more units into operation, it usually shortens the dispatch interval, so more units are being dispatched more often.

5. *How many staff personnel are available to operate the ride.* Allocation of additional staff to a given ride can allow extra units to be placed in operation, or additional loading areas or holding areas to be opened. Pirates of the Caribbean and It's a Small World can run two separate waiting lines and loading zones. Haunted Mansion has a short "pre-show" which is staged in a "stretch room." On busy days a second "stretch room" can be activated, thus permitting a more continuous flow of visitors to the actual loading area. Additional staff make a world of difference on some cycle rides. Often, if not usually, one attendant will operate the Mad Tea Party. This single person must clear the visitors from the ride just completed, admit and seat visitors for the upcoming ride, check that all Tea Cups are properly secured (which entails an inspection of each Tea Cup), return to the control panel, issue instructions to the riders, and finally, activate the ride (whew!). A second attendant allows for the division of these responsibilities and has the effect of cutting loading time by 25 to 50 percent.

—— *Saving Time in Line*
by Understanding the Shows ——

Many of the featured attractions at Disneyland are theater presentations. While not as complex from a traffic engineering viewpoint as rides, a little enlightenment concerning their operation may save some touring time.

Most of the theater attractions at Disneyland operate in three distinct phases:

1. First there are the visitors who are in the theater viewing the presentation.

2. Next there are the visitors who have passed through the turnstile into a holding area or waiting lobby. These people will be admitted to the theater as soon as the current presentation is concluded. Several attractions offer a "pre-show" in their waiting lobby to entertain the crowd until they are admitted to the main show. Among these are the World Premier Circle-Vision and *Captain EO*.

3. Finally there is the outside line. Visitors waiting here will enter the waiting lobby when there is room, and then be moved into the theater when the audience turns over (is exchanged) between shows.

PART TWO—Tips and Warnings

—— Credit Cards ——

- American Express, MasterCard, and VISA are accepted for theme park admission.

- *No credit cards* are accepted in the theme park at fast-food restaurants.

- Disneyland shops, sit-down restaurants, and the Disneyland Hotel will accept American Express, MasterCard, and VISA credit cards.

—— Rain ——

If it rains, go anyway; the bad weather will serve to diminish the crowds. Additionally, most of the rides and attractions in Disneyland are under cover. Likewise, all but a few of the waiting areas are protected from inclement weather. If you get caught by an unexpected downpour, rain gear of varying sorts can be purchased at a number of Disneyland shops.

—— Small Children ——

We believe that children should be a fairly mature eight years old to really *appreciate* Disneyland, though children of almost any age will *enjoy* it.

A Word About the Rides. All of the roller coaster rides and several other rides have a minimum height and age requirement to ride. Generally, a child must be 3'4" tall **and** at least three years old to experience these rides. Somewhere near the entrance to the specified rides, and often hidden by the waiting lines, will be a marker that a child can measure up against to determine if he is tall enough. If you are touring

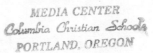

with a child who wishes to enjoy the rides in question, have him measured before you stand in line. If you get in line first, you may stand in line for a long time before you reach the marker. If your child isn't tall enough you will be asked to leave the line. Rides with height requirements are:

Frontierland	Big Thunder Mountain Railroad
Fantasyland	Motor Boat Cruise
	Fantasyland Autopia
	Matterhorn Bobsleds
Tomorrowland	Space Mountain
	Tomorrowland Autopia

Disneyland is a family theme park. Yet some of the Disney adventure rides can be intimidating to small children. On certain rides such as the roller coaster rides (Space Mountain, Matterhorn Bobsleds, and Big Thunder Mountain Railroad), the ride itself may be frightening. On other rides such as the Haunted Mansion and Snow White's Scary Adventures, it is the special effects. We recommend a little parent-child dialogue coupled with a "testing the water" approach. A child who is frightened by Pinocchio's Daring Journey should not have to sit through the Haunted Mansion. Likewise, if Big Thunder Mountain Railroad was too much, don't try Space Mountain or the Matterhorn Bobsleds.

Disney, Kids, and Scary Stuff. Disney rides and shows are adventures. They focus on the substance and themes of all adventure, and indeed of life itself: good and evil, quest, death, beauty and the grotesque, fellowship and enmity. As you sample the variety of attractions at Disneyland, you transcend the mundane spinning and bouncing of midway rides to a more thought-provoking and emotionally powerful entertainment experience. Though the endings are all happy, the impact of the adventures, with Disney's gift for special effects, is often intimidating and occasionally frightening to small children.

There are rides with menacing witches, rides with burning towns, and rides with ghouls popping out of their graves, all done tongue-in-cheek and with a sense of humor, providing you are old enough to understand the joke. And bones, lot of bones; human bones, cattle bones, dinosaur bones, and whole skeletons everywhere you look. There have got to be more bones at Disneyland than at the Smithsonian Institute and UCLA Medical School combined. There is a stack of skulls at the headhunter's camp on the Jungle Cruise, a veritable platoon of skeletons sailing ghost ships in Pirates of the Caribbean, a haunting assemblage of skulls and skeletons in the Haunted Mansion, with more skulls, skeletons, and bones punctuating Snow White's Scary Adventures, Peter Pan's Flight, and Big Thunder Mountain Railroad, to name a few.

Most small children take Disney's variety of macabre trappings in stride, and others are quickly comforted by an arm around the shoulder or a little squeeze of the hand. But for those kids whose parents have observed a tendency to become upset when exposed to such sights, we recommend taking it slow and easy, sampling more benign adventures like the Jungle Cruise, gauging reactions, and discussing with the children how they felt about the things they saw.

A Little Bit at a Time.   Small children often become tired and irritable after several hours of standing in line and being jostled among the crowds. If your schedule allows, we recommend touring Disneyland in small doses. Go early in the morning and tour until about lunch time. Go back to your hotel for some food and maybe a nap. Return later in the evening or on the morning of the following day.

Strollers—are available for rent at a modest fee. For non-walking infants and toddlers the strollers are a must. We observed several sharp parents renting strollers for somewhat older children (up to 4 or 5 years). Having the stroller precluded having to carry the child when he ran out of steam and also afforded a place for the child to sit during long waits in line. Strollers can be obtained at the right of the entrance to Disneyland (at the base of the Main Street Train Station). NOTE: Sometimes strollers disappear while you are enjoying a ride or a show. Do not be alarmed: you will not have to buy the missing stroller and you will be issued a new stroller for your continued use.

Baby-Sitting.   Many of the hotels in the Disneyland area provide baby-sitter referrals. Inquire when you make your reservations.

Caring for Infants and Toddlers.   Disneyland has special centralized facilities for the care of infants and toddlers. Everything necessary for changing diapers, preparing formulas, warming bottles and food, etc., is available in ample quantity. A broad selection of baby supplies is on hand for sale and there are even rockers and special chairs for nursing mothers. The Baby Center is located next to the Carefree Corner at the central hub end of Main Street.

Lost Children. Lost children normally do not present much of a problem at Disneyland. All Disney employees are schooled to handle the situation should it be encountered. If you lose a child while touring, report the situation to a Disney employ, and then check in at the Baby Center and at City Hall where lost children "logs" are maintained. There are no paging systems at Disneyland, but in an emergency an "all points bulletin" can be issued throughout the park via internal communications. For your peace of mind, special name tags can be obtained to aid in identification should a child become separated from his party.

—— *Visitors with Special Needs* ——

Handicapped visitors. Rental wheelchairs are available if needed. Most rides, shows, attractions, restrooms, and restaurants are engineered to accommodate the handicapped. For specific inquiries or problems call (714) 999-4565. If you are in Disneyland and need some special assistance, go to City Hall on Main Street. Close-in parking is available for the handicapped; inquire when you pay your parking fee.

Foreign Language Assistance—available to non-English-speaking guests. Inquire by calling (714) 999-4565 or by stopping in at City Hall or at Guest Relations to the right of the Main Entrance.

Lost Adults. Arrange a plan for regrouping with those in your party should you become separated. Failing this, you can leave a message at City Hall for your missing person.

Messages—can be left at City Hall.

Car Trouble. If the problem is simple, one of the security patrols which continually cruise the parking lots might be able to put you back in business. Otherwise, phone one of the nearby service stations.

Lost and Found. If you lose (or find) something, the lost and found office is located next to the Emporium at the City Square end of Main Street. If you do not discover your loss until you have left the park, call (714) 999-4565.

— *Excuse Me, But Where Can I Find* . . .

Someplace to Put All These Packages?   Lockers are available at the Town Square end of Main Street next to the Emporium.

A Mixed Drink or Beer?   If you are in Disneyland you are out of luck. You will have to exit the park and try one of the hotels.

Some Rain Gear?   If you get caught in a rare California monsoon, here's where you can find something to cover up with:

Main Street:	The Emporium
Tomorrowland:	Character Shop
Fantasyland:	Mad Hatter
Frontierland:	Frontier Trading Post

A Cure for This Headache?   Aspirin and various other sundries can be purchased on Main Street at the Emporium (they keep them behind the counter so you have to ask).

A Prescription Filled?   Unfortunately, there is no place in Disneyland to have a prescription filled.

Suntan Lotion?   Suntan lotion and various other sundries can be purchased on Main Street at the Emporium (they keep them behind the counter so you have to ask).

A Smoke?   Cigarettes are readily available throughout Disneyland.

Main Street:	The Tobacco Shop
New Orleans Square:	Marché aux Fleurs
Bear Country:	Wilderness Outpost
Frontierland:	Frontier Rock Shop
Tomorrowland:	Character Shop

Feminine Hygiene Products?   Feminine hygiene products are available in most of the women's restrooms at Disneyland.

Cash? A branch of the Bank of America is located on Main Street next to *The Walt Disney Story* at the Town Square end. The following services are offered:

— *Cash advances on Mastercard and VISA credit cards* ($50.00 minimum, with a maximum equaling the patron's credit limit).

— *Personal checks* may be cashed for $25.00 or less if drawn on U.S. banks; presentation of a valid driver's license and a major credit card is required.

— *Cash and sale of traveler's checks.* Refunds are provided for lost American Express and Bank of America traveler's checks.

— *Wire money* from the visitor's bank to the Bank of America.

— *Exchange of foreign currency* for dollars.

A Place to Leave My Pet? Cooping up an animal in a hot car while you tour can lead to disastrous results. Additionally, pets are not allowed in Disneyland (except seeing eye dogs). Kennels and holding facilities are provided for the temporary care of your pets and are located to the right of the Main Entrance. If you are adamant, the folks at the kennels will accept custody of just about any type of animal. Owners of pets, exotic or otherwise, must themselves place their charge in the assigned cage. Small pets (mice, hamsters, birds, snakes, turtles, alligators, etc.) must arrive in their own escape-proof quarters.

In addition to the above, there are several other details which you may need to know:

— Advance reservations for animals are not accepted.

— Kennels open one hour before the theme parks open and close one hour after the theme parks close.

— Pets may not be boarded overnight.

— Guests leaving exotic pets should supply food for their pet.

— On busy days there is a one to two hour bottleneck at the kennel, beginning a half hour before the park opens. If you need to use the kennel on such a day, arrive at least an hour before the park's stated opening time.

Film? Film may be purchased at the Emporium on Main Street, as well as at other shops throughout the park.

—— *How to Deal with Obnoxious People* ——

At every theater presentation at Disneyland, visitors in the pre-show area elbow, nudge, and crowd one another in order to make sure that they are admitted to the performance. Not necessary—if you are admitted through the turnstile into the preshow area a seat has auto-matically been allocated for you in the theater. When it is time to proceed into the theater don't rush; just relax and let other people jam the doorways. When the congestion has been relieved simply stroll in and take a seat.

Attendants at many theaters will instruct you to enter a row of seats and move completely to the far side, filling every seat so that each row can be completely filled. And invariably some inconsiderate, thick-skulled yahoo will plop down right in the middle of the row, stopping traffic or forcing other visitors to climb over him. Take our word for it —there is no such thing as a bad seat. All of the Disney theaters have been designed to provide a near perfect view from every seat in the house. Our recommendation is to follow instructions and move to the far end of the row, and if you encounter some dummy blocking the middle of the row, have every person in your party step very hard on his toes as you move past him.

The Disney people also ask that visitors not use flash photography in the theaters (the theaters are too dark for the pictures to turn out, *plus* the flash is disruptive to other viewers). Needless to say, this admoni-tion is routinely ignored. Flashers are more difficult to deal with than row-blockers. You can threaten to turn the offenders over to Disney Security, or better yet, simply hold your hand over the lens (you have to be quick) when they raise their cameras.

PART THREE—Disneyland in Detail

—— Arriving and Getting Oriented ——

Disneyland and its parking lot occupy a huge city block. If you drive, parking costs a dollar, and a tram will carry you to the main entrance ticket booths. Stroller and wheelchair rentals are to the right just beyond the turnstile. Entering Main Street, City Hall is to your left, serving as the center for information, lost and found, and entertainment information. To the right of City Hall is the Fire Station, and to its right are rental lockers for your use.

If you haven't been given a guide to Disneyland by now, City Hall is the place to pick one up. The guide contains maps, gives tips for good photos, lists all the attractions, shops, and eating places, and provides helpful information about first aid, baby care, assistance for the handicapped, and more.

While at City Hall inquire about special events, live entertainment, Disney Character parades, concerts, and other activities scheduled for that day. Sometimes City Hall will have a little printed schedule to provide you. Other days no printed handouts are available and you will have to take a few notes.

Notice on your map that Main Street ends at a central hub from which branch the entrances to four other sections of Disneyland: Adventureland, Frontierland, Fantasyland, and Tomorrowland. Two other "lands," New Orleans Square and Bear Country, can be reached through Adventureland and Frontierland. Sleeping Beauty's Castle serves as the entrance to Fantasyland and is a focal landmark and visual center of the park. The Castle is a great place to meet if your group decides to split up for any reason during the day, and it can serve as an emergency meeting place if you are accidentally separated.

Starting the Tour

Everyone will soon find his or her own favorite and not-so-favorite attractions in Disneyland. Be open-minded and adventuresome. Don't dismiss a particular ride or show as being not for you until AFTER you have tried it. Our personal experience as well as our research indicates that each visitor is different in terms of which Disney offerings he most enjoys. So don't miss seeing an attraction because a friend from home didn't like it; that attraction may turn out to be your favorite.

We do recommend that you take advantage of what Disney does best—the fantasy adventures like the Jungle Cruise and the Haunted Mansion, and the AudioAnimatronic (talking robots, so to speak) attractions such as the Pirates of the Caribbean. Unless you have almost unlimited time, don't burn a lot of daylight browsing through the shops. Except for some special Disney souvenirs, you can find most of the same merchandise elsewhere. Try to minimize the time you spend on carnival-type rides; you've probably got an amusement park, carnival, or state fair closer to your hometown. Don't, however, mistake rides like Space Mountain and the Big Thunder Mountain Railway as being amusement park rides. They may be of the roller coaster genre, but they represent pure Disney genius. Similarly, do not devote a lot of time to waiting in lines for meals. Food at most Disneyland eateries is mediocre and uninspiring at best. Eat a good early breakfast before you come, snack on vendor-sold foods during the touring day, or follow the suggestions for meals incorporated into the various Touring Plans presented.

Main Street, USA

This section of Disneyland is where you'll begin and end your visit. We have already mentioned that assistance and information are available at City Hall. The Disneyland Railroad stops at the Main Street Station, and you can board here for a grand circle tour of the park, or you can get off the train in New Orleans Square or Tomorrowland.

Main Street is a replication of a turn-of-the-century American small-town street. Many visitors are surprised to discover that all the buildings are real as opposed to being elaborate props. Attention to detail here is exceptional—interiors, furnishings, and fixtures conform to the period. As with any real Main Street, the Disney version is essentially a collection of shops and eating places, with a City Hall, a Fire Station, and an old-time cinema. A mixed-media attraction combines a presentation on the life of Walt Disney (*The Walt Disney Story*) with a patriotic remembrance of Abraham Lincoln. Horse-drawn trolleys, fire engines, and horseless carriages give rides along Main Street and transport visitors to the central hub (properly known as Plaza Hub).

—— *Main Street Services* ——

Most of the park's service facilities are centered in the Main Street section, including the following:

Wheelchair and Stroller Rental	To the right of the main entrance before passing under the Railroad Station
Banking Services/ Currency Exchange	To the right of *The Walt Disney Story* at the Railroad Station end of Main Street
Storage Lockers	To the right of the Fire Station at the Railroad Station end of Main Street
Lost & Found	To the right of the Fire Station at the Railroad Station end of Main Street

49

Main Street Services (continued)

Live Entertainment & Parade Information	City Hall Building at the Railroad Station end of Main Street
Lost Persons	City Hall Building
Disneyland & Local Attraction Information	City Hall and Carefree Corner at the central hub end of Main Street on the right
First Aid	First Aid Center two doors from the Carefree Corner at the central hub end of Main Street
Baby Center/Baby Care Needs	Next door to the Carefree Corner

—— *Main Street Attractions* ——

Disneyland Railroad

Type of Attraction: Scenic railroad ride around the perimeter of
   Disneyland; also transportation to New Orleans Square and
   Tomorrowland

When to Go: After 11 A.M. or when you need transportation

Special Comments: Main Street Station is usually the least congested
   boarding point

Authors' Rating: ★★★★ [Critical ratings are based on a scale of zero
   to five stars. Five stars is the best possible rating.]

Overall Appeal by Age Group:

Pre- school	Grade School	Teens	Young Adults	Over 30	Senior Citizens
★★★★	★★★★	★★★★	★★★★	★★★★	★★★★

Duration of Ride: About 17 minutes for a complete circuit

Average Wait in Line per 100 People Ahead of You: 8 minutes

Assumes: 3 trains operating

Loading Speed: Fast

DESCRIPTION AND COMMENTS   A transportation ride which blends an
unusual variety of sights and experiences with an energy-saving way of
getting around the park. In addition to providing a glimpse of all the
lands except Adventureland, the train passes through the Grand Can-

yon Diorama, a three-dimensional replication of the canyon, complete with wildlife, as it appears from the southern rim. A more recent addition to the train circuit is Primeval World, a depiction of a prehistoric peat bog and rain forest populated by AudioAnimatronic (robotic) dinosaurs. Opened in 1966, the display was a precursor to a similar presentation in the Universe of Energy pavilion at EPCOT Center.

TOURING TIPS   Save the train ride until after you have seen the featured attractions, or use it when you need transportation. On busy days lines form at the New Orleans Square and Tomorrowland Stations, but rarely at the Main Street Station.

The Walt Disney Story *Featuring*
Great Moments with Mr. Lincoln

Type of Attraction: Nostalgic look at the Disney success story
    followed by a patriotic presentation
When to Go: During the hot, crowded period of the day
Authors' Rating: Both presentations are very moving; ★★★★
Overall Appeal by Age Group:

Pre-school	Grade School	Teens	Young Adults	Over 30	Senior Citizens
★★½	★★★	★★★	★★★½	★★★★½	★★★★½

Duration of Presentation: Disney Story: 7 minutes
                            Great Moments: 13 minutes
Pre-Show Entertainment: Disney exhibits
Probable Waiting Time: Usually no wait

DESCRIPTION AND COMMENTS   A warm and well-produced remembrance of the man who started it all. Well worth seeing, especially touching for those old enough to remember Walt Disney. The attraction consists of a museum of Disney memorabilia, including a re-creation of Walt's office and a seven-minute film about Walt Disney. Especially interesting are displays illustrating the construction and evolution of Disneyland. Following the conclusion of the film about Walt Disney, guests are admitted to a large theater where *Great Moments with Mr. Lincoln* is presented. A patriotic performance, *Great Moments* features an extremely lifelike and sophisticated AudioAnimatronic Lincoln delivering some well-considered thoughts concerning the past and the future of the United States.

Walt Disney Story (continued)

TOURING TIPS   You usually do not have to wait long for this show, so see it during the busy times of the day when lines are long elsewhere or as you are leaving the park.

Main Street Cinema

Type of Attraction: Old time movies and vintage Disney cartoons
When to Go: Whenever you want
Authors' Rating: Wonderful selection of hilarious flicks; ★★★½
Overall Appeal by Age Group:

Pre-school	Grade School	Teens	Young Adults	Over 30	Senior Citizens
★★½	★★★	★★★	★★★½	★★★½	★★★½

Duration of Presentation: Runs continuously
Pre-Show Entertainment: None
Probable Waiting Time: No waiting

DESCRIPTION AND COMMENTS   Excellent old time movies including some vintage Disney cartoons. Since the movies are silent, six can be shown simultaneously. No seats, viewers stand.

TOURING TIPS   Good place to get out of the sun or rain or to kill time while others in your group shop on Main Street. Fun, but not something you can't afford to miss.

—— Main Street Restaurants and Shops ——

DESCRIPTION AND COMMENTS   Mediocre food, and specialty/souvenir shopping in a nostalgic, happy setting.

Incidentally, the Emporium on Main Street and the Character Shop in Tomorrowland are the two best places for finding Disney trademark souvenirs.

TOURING TIPS   The shops are fun but the merchandise can be had elsewhere (except for certain Disney Trademark souvenirs). If seeing the park attractions is your objective, save the Main Street eateries and shops until the end of the day. If shopping is your objective, you will find the shops most crowded during the noon hour and near closing time. Remember, Main Street opens at least a half hour earlier, and closes a half hour to an hour later than the rest of Disneyland.

—— *Main Street Minor Attractions* ——

Transportation Rides

DESCRIPTION AND COMMENTS   Trolleys, buses, etc., which add color to Main Street.

TOURING TIPS   Will save you a walk to the central hub. Not worth waiting in line for.

Penny Arcade

DESCRIPTION AND COMMENTS   The Penny Arcade features some vintage arcade machines which can actually be played for a penny or a nickel. Located toward the central hub end of Main Street on the left as you face the Castle.

TOURING TIPS   If you arrive early when Main Street is the only part of the park open, you might want to spend a few minutes here.

Disneyland Showcase

DESCRIPTION AND COMMENTS   The Disneyland Showcase, located on the right corner as you start down Main Street from Town Square, features exhibits documenting the past and future of the Disney theme parks and provides promos and previews of Disney movies.

TOURING TIPS   Usually interesting and a good place to kill a few minutes waiting for the rest of the park to open or for a parade to begin.

Adventureland

Adventureland is the first "land" to the left of Main Street and embodies a safari/African motif.

Enchanted Tiki Room

Type of Attraction: AudioAnimatronic Pacific Island musical show
When to Go: Before 11 A.M. and after 6 P.M.
Authors' Rating: Very, very unusual; ★★★½
Overall Appeal by Age Group:

Pre-school	Grade School	Teens	Young Adults	Over 30	Senior Citizens
★★½	★★★	★★	★★★½	★★★½	★★★½

Duration of Presentation: 16½ minutes
Pre-Show Entertainment: Talking totem poles
Probable Waiting Time: 15 minutes

DESCRIPTION AND COMMENTS   An unusual sit-down theater performance where more than 200 birds, flowers, and Tiki-god statues sing and whistle through a musical program.

TOURING TIPS   One of the more bizarre of the Disneyland entertainments and sometimes very crowded. We like it in the early evening when we can especially appreciate sitting for a bit in an air-conditioned theater.

Jungle Cruise

Type of Ride: A Disney boat ride adventure
When to Go: Before 10 A.M. or after 6 P.M.
Authors' Rating: A long enduring Disney masterpiece; ★★★★

Jungle Cruise (*continued*)

Overall Appeal by Age Group:

Pre-school	Grade School	Teens	Young Adults	Over 30	Senior Citizens
★★★★★	★★★★★	★★★★	★★★★½	★★★★½	★★★★½

Duration of Ride: 8–9 minutes

Average Wait in Line per 100 People Ahead of You: 3½ minutes

Assumes: 10 boats operating

Loading Speed: Moderate

DESCRIPTION AND COMMENTS   A boat ride through jungle waterways. Passengers encounter elephants, lions, hostile natives, and a menacing hippo. A long enduring Disney favorite, with the boatman's spiel adding measurably to the fun.

TOURING TIPS   One of the park's "not to be missed" attractions. Go early: this ride loads slowly and long lines form as the park fills. Also, much of the waiting area is exposed to the elements.

Swiss Family Treehouse

Type of Attraction: Walk-through exhibit

When to Go: Before 11 A.M. and after 5 P.M.

Special Comments: Requires climbing a lot of stairs

Authors' Rating: A very creative exhibit; ★★★★

Overall Appeal by Age Group:

Pre-school	Grade School	Teens	Young Adults	Over 30	Senior Citizens
★★★★	★★★★	★★★★	★★★★	★★★★	★★★★

Duration of Tour: 4–8 minutes

Average Wait in Line per 100 People Ahead of You: 7 minutes

Assumes: Normal staffing

Loading Speed: Does not apply

DESCRIPTION AND COMMENTS   A fantastic replication of the shipwrecked family's home will fire the imagination of the inventive and the adventurous.

Swiss Family Treehouse (continued)

TOURING TIPS   A self-guided walk-through tour which involves a lot of climbing up and down stairs but no ropes or ladders or anything fancy. People stopping during the walk-through to look extra long or to rest sometimes create bottlenecks which slow crowd flow. We recommend visiting this attraction in the late afternoon or early evening if you are on a one-day tour schedule.

—— Adventureland Shops and Eateries ——

DESCRIPTION AND COMMENTS   More specialty shopping and mediocre food for the most part. An exception is Tahitian Terrace, which serves palatable food and puts on a whale of a dinner show featuring South Sea Island dancing and music. Seating for the shows is first come, first serve. If you want to insure a seat, arrive an hour or more early. Information concerning show times is available at the restaurant and usually at City Hall. No lunch show.

TOURING TIPS   Skip the shops and eateries unless you specifically came to shop and eat, or try them on your second day. The Tahitian Terrace, unbeknownst to many, is open for lunch (with no show). Sometimes, you can eat here more quickly than you can at neighboring fast-food lines.

New Orleans Square

Accessible via Adventureland and Frontierland, New Orleans Square is one of two lands which do not emanate from the central hub. The architecture and setting are Caribbean colonial, with exceptional attention to detail.

Pirates of the Caribbean

Type of Ride: A Disney adventure boat ride
When to Go: Before 11 A.M. and after 6 P.M.
Special Comments: This ride frightens some small children.
Authors' Rating: Our pick as best attraction at Disneyland; ★★★★★
Overall Appeal by Age Group:

Pre-school	Grade School	Teens	Young Adults	Over 30	Senior Citizens
★★★	★★★★★	★★★★★	★★★★★	★★★★★	★★★★★

Duration of Ride: Approximately 14 minutes
Average Wait in Line per 100 People Ahead of You: 3 minutes
Assumes: 42 boats operating
Loading Speed: Fast

DESCRIPTION AND COMMENTS   Another boat ride, this time indoors, through a series of sets depicting a pirate raid on an island settlement, from the bombardment of the fortress to the debauchery which follows the victory. All in good, clean fun.

TOURING TIPS   Another "not to be missed" attraction. Undoubtedly one of the most elaborate and imaginative attractions in Disneyland. Engineered to move large crowds in a hurry, Pirates nevertheless forms lines of startling proportions. Try to see this attraction before 11 A.M. or from 6 P.M. until closing.

Disneyland Railroad

DESCRIPTION AND COMMENTS   The Disneyland Railroad stops in New Orleans Square on its circle tour around the park. See the description of the Disneyland Railroad under Main Street for additional details regarding the sights en route.

TOURING TIPS   A pleasant and feet-saving way to commute to Tomorrowland and/or Main Street. Be advised, however, that the New Orleans Square Station is usually the most congested.

Haunted Mansion

Type of Ride: A Disney one-of-its-kind
When to Go: Before 11:30 A.M. or after 6:30 P.M.
Special Comments: This ride frightens some very small children.
Authors' Rating: Some of Disneyland's best special effects; ★★★★★
Overall Appeal by Age Group:

Pre- school	Grade School	Teens	Young Adults	Over 30	Senior Citizens
Varies	★★★★½	★★★★½	★★★★½	★★★★½	★★★★½

Duration of Ride: 5½-minute ride plus a two-minute pre-show
Average Wait in Line per 100 People Ahead of You: 2½ minutes
Assumes: Both stretch rooms operating
Loading Speed: Fast

DESCRIPTION AND COMMENTS   A fun attraction more than a scary one, with some of the best special effects in Disneyland. In their Souvenir guide the Disney people say, "Come face to face with 999 happy ghosts, ghouls, and goblins in a 'frightfully funny' adventure." That pretty well sums it up. Be warned that some youngsters build a lot of anxiety concerning what they think they will see. The actual attraction scares almost nobody.

TOURING TIPS   This attraction would be more at home in Fantasyland, but no matter, it's Disney at its best; another "not to be missed" feature. Try to see the Mansion before 11:15 A.M. or after 5:30 P.M.

—— *New Orleans Square Eateries and Shops* ——

DESCRIPTION AND COMMENTS   Shops and restaurants in New Orleans Square impart a special realism to the setting. The Blue Bayou Restaurant, situated left of the Pirates of the Caribbean ride exit, offers an exotic, romantic atmosphere equaled by few restaurants anywhere.

TOURING TIPS   Skip the restaurants and shops if you have only one or two days to visit. If you have some extra time, however, treat yourself to a meal at the Blue Bayou Restaurant. The food is a cut above the usual Disney fare and the atmosphere will knock you out. Reservations are accepted for the evening meal as of 2 P.M.

Bear Country

Bear Country, situated at the end of a cul de sac, and accessible via New Orleans Square, sports a pioneer appearance not unlike that of Frontierland.

Country Bear Jamboree

Type of Attraction: AudioAnimatronic country hoedown stage show
When to Go: After 11 A.M. and before 5 P.M.
Authors' Rating: A Disney classic, not to be missed; ★★★★½
Overall Appeal by Age Group:

Pre-school	Grade School	Teens	Young Adults	Over 30	Senior Citizens
★★★★	★★★★	★★★★	★★★★½	★★★★½	★★★★½

Duration of Presentation: 15 minutes
Pre-Show Entertainment: None
Probable Waiting Time: 5–10 minutes

DESCRIPTION AND COMMENTS   A cast of charming AudioAnimatronic (robotic) bears sing and stomp their way through a Western-style hoedown. One of Disneyland's most humorous and upbeat shows.

TOURING TIPS   Yet another "not to be missed" attraction, the *Jamboree* is extremely popular but is one of the most efficient crowd movers in the park. Try the *Jamboree* between 11 A.M. and 5:30 P.M.

Davy Crockett's Explorer Canoes

Type of ride: Scenic canoe ride
When to Go: Before 11 A.M.
Special Comments: Skip if the lines are long. Closes at dusk.
Authors' Rating: Most fun way of seeing Rivers of America; ★★★★

Davy Crockett's Explorer Canoes (continued)

Overall Appeal by Age Group:

Pre-school	Grade School	Teens	Young Adults	Over 30	Senior Citizens
★★★★	★★★★	★★★★	★★★★	★★★★	★★★★

Duration of Ride: 8–10 minutes depending on how fast you paddle

Average Wait in Line per 100 People Ahead of You: 12½ minutes

Assumes: 6 canoes operating

Loading Speed: Slow

DESCRIPTION AND COMMENTS   Paddle-powered (your paddle) ride around Tom Sawyer Island and Fort Wilderness. Runs the same route with the same sights as the Steamboat, the Sailing Ship, and the Mike Fink Keel Boats. The canoes only operate on busier days and close at dusk. The sights are fun and the ride is a little different in that the patrons paddle the canoe. We think this is the most fun of any of the various river trips. Long lines from about 11 A.M. on reflect the popularity of this attraction.

TOURING TIPS   The canoes represent one of four ways to see the same waterways. Since the canoes and keel boats are slower loading, we usually opt for the larger Steamboat or Sailing Ship. If you are not up for a boat ride, a different view of the same sights can be had by hoofing around Tom Sawyer Island and Fort Wilderness. Try to ride before 11 A.M. or just before dusk.

—— Bear Country Eateries and Shops ——

DESCRIPTION AND COMMENTS   Bear Country restaurants and shops offer the standard array of souvenirs and fast food.

TOURING TIPS   Bear Country is in an isolated, far corner of Disneyland and contains only one ride and one show. Given its location and comparatively modest offering of attractions, it tends to be a little less crowded than neighboring New Orleans Square or Frontierland. What all this means is that Bear Country's two fast-food restaurants are often good bets for avoiding the lunch rush, especially if you arrive before 11:45 A.M.

Frontierland

Frontierland adjoins New Orleans Square as you move clockwise around the park. The focus here is on the Old West, with stockades and pioneer trappings.

Big Thunder Mountain Railroad

Type of Ride: Tame roller coaster with exciting special effects

When to Go: The first hour the park is open, between 10 and 11 A.M., when carrying capacity is increased, and the hour before closing

Special Comments: Children must be 3'4" tall to ride. Those under 7 years must ride with an adult.

Authors' Rating: Great effects/relatively tame ride; ★★★★

Overall Appeal by Age Group:

Pre-school	Grade School	Teens	Young Adults	Over 30	Senior Citizens
★★★	★★★★	★★★★	★★★★	★★★★	★★★★

Duration of Ride: 3⅓ minutes

Average Wait in Line per 100 People Ahead of You: 3 minutes

Assumes: 5 trains operating

Loading Speed: Moderate to fast

DESCRIPTION AND COMMENTS   A roller coaster ride through and around a Disney "mountain." The time is Gold Rush days, and the idea is that you are on a runaway mine train. Along with the usual thrills of a roller coaster ride (about a 5 on a "scary scale" of 10), the ride showcases some first-rate examples of Disney creativity: lifelike scenes depicting a mining town, falling rocks, and an earthquake, all humorously animated.

TOURING TIPS   A superb Disney experience, but not too wild a roller coaster. The emphasis here is much more on the sights than on the thrill of the ride itself. Regardless, it's a "not to be missed" attraction. The best bet for riding Big Thunder without a long wait in line is to ride early in the morning or between 10 and 11 A.M. when the ride has been brought up to peak carrying capacity.

Big Thunder Ranch

Type of Attraction: Walk-through ranch and petting zoo
When to Go: Anytime
Special Comments: Animals are real.
Authors' Rating: Something different for Disney; ★★½
Overall Appeal by Age Group:

Pre-school	Grade School	Teens	Young Adults	Over 30	Senior Citizens
★★★★	★★★½	★★	★★½	★★½	★★½

Duration of Tour: 5–10 minutes
Average Wait in Line per 100 People Ahead of You: Usually no waiting though petting zoo gets congested on busier days

DESCRIPTION AND COMMENTS   Big Thunder Ranch is a replica of an old Western homestead complete with a walk-through log cabin, a blacksmith shop and a corral that serves as a petting zoo. Located on a path that winds from Frontierland to Fantasyland around the rear of Big Thunder Mountain, the Ranch seems to be more of a space-filler than a true-blue Disney attraction. The petting zoo is small and the cabin can accommodate only a handful of visitors at a time. Anyone who likes animals, however, will enjoy the clean, well-maintained petting zoo, and adults touring with children will find the Ranch a nice rest stop.

TOURING TIPS   Visit anytime as your schedule allows, but don't waste time here waiting in line. If the Ranch is too crowded for you to just walk in, skip it.

Golden Horseshoe Revue

Type of Attraction: Live song/dance/comedy stage show
When to Go: As per your reservations
Special Comments: Seating by reservation only, made on the day of the show. Lunch is available.
Authors' Rating: Good show but not worth all the hassle; ★★★½
Overall Appeal by Age Group:

Pre-school	Grade School	Teens	Young Adults	Over 30	Senior Citizens
★★½	★★★	★★★★	★★★★	★★★★	★★★★

Golden Horseshoe Revue (*continued*)

Duration of Presentation: About 20 minutes
Pre-Show Entertainment: 5 minutes
Probable Waiting Time: See Touring Tips

DESCRIPTION AND COMMENTS   A half-hour, G-rated re-creation of an Old West dance-hall show, with dancing, singing, and lots of corny comedy. Patrons are seated at tables where snacks, sandwiches, and non-alcoholic drinks can be ordered before the show. This is a good performance, but you can see this sort of entertainment with far less effort elsewhere.

TOURING TIPS   Though we acknowledge the quality of the show, we recommend that this attraction be skipped unless you have at least two full days to devote to Disneyland. Here's why: Seating is by reservation only, made in person on the day you want to see the show. To obtain a reservation you have to run first thing in the morning to the Golden Horseshoe Saloon and stand in line when you could be hopping on any ride you liked without much if any waiting. Reservation lines move very slowly because every patron needs to ask questions and receive instructions. If you are able to obtain a reservation for one of the several shows, you will be required to return for seating 45 minutes before show time when you will wait in line again (this time to be admitted to the theater). Once allowed inside you will wait for another half hour or so for food orders to be taken and processed before the show finally begins. By observation and experimentation we have determined that a Disneyland patron spends an average of one hour making his reservation, and 45 minutes waiting for the show to begin, and he has to adjust his other touring plans—to be back in Frontierland in time to be seated. Thus, counting the show itself, a two-hour-and-fifteen-minute investment of valuable time to see a 30-minute song and dance show. We recommend seeing the show only on your second day. Follow the instructions for Day Two of the Disneyland Two-Day Touring Plan.

Raft to and from Tom Sawyer Island

Type of Ride: Transportation ride to Tom Sawyer Island
Special Comments: Same information applies to return trip
Duration of Ride: A little over a minute one way
Average Wait in Line per 100 People Ahead of You: $4\frac{1}{2}$ minutes

Assumes: Three rafts operating

Loading Speed: Moderate

Tom Sawyer Island & Fort Wilderness

Type of Attraction: Walk-through exhibit/rustic playground

When to Go: Mid-morning through late afternoon

Special Comments: Closes at dusk; muddy following a hard rain

Authors' Rating: The place for rambunctious kids; ★★★★

Overall Appeal by Age Group:

Pre-school	Grade School	Teens	Young Adults	Over 30	Senior Citizens
★★★★★	★★★★★	★★★½	★★★	★★★	★★★

DESCRIPTION AND COMMENTS Tom Sawyer Island manages to impart something of a sense of isolation from the rest of the park. It has hills to climb, a cave and a treehouse to explore, tipsy bridges to cross, and paths to follow. It's a delight for adults but a godsend for children who have been in tow all day. They love the freedom of the exploration and the excitement of firing air guns from the walls of Fort Wilderness. There's even a "secret" escape tunnel. Be advised that due to the scuffling of millions of tiny feet there is not a blade of grass left intact on the entire island. Thus, after a good rain, Tom Sawyer Island is miraculously transformed into Disney's Muddy Wallow. Parents should feel free within reasonable limits to allow their children to explore unfettered. In addition to the fact that the island is designed for rowdy kids, there are a goodly number of Disney security people (dressed as cavalry soldiers) to referee the transient cowboys and Indians.

TOURING TIPS Tom Sawyer Island is not one of Disneyland's more celebrated attractions, but it's certainly one of the best done. Attention to detail is excellent and kids particularly revel in its adventuresome frontier atmosphere. We think it's a must for families with children five through fifteen. If your party is adult, visit the island on your second day, or stop by on your first day if you have seen the attractions you most wanted to see. We like Tom Sawyer Island from about noon until the island closes at dusk. Access is by raft from Frontierland, and you may have to stand in line to board both coming and going. Two or three rafts operate simultaneously, however, and the round trip is usually pretty time efficient. Tom Sawyer Island takes about 35 minutes or so to see, but many children could spend a whole day.

Frontierland Shooting Arcade

Type of Attraction: Lead pellet shooting gallery

When to Go: Whenever convenient

Special Comments: Costs fifty cents per play

Authors' Rating: A very nifty shooting gallery; ★★★½

Overall Appeal by Age Group:

Pre-school	Grade School	Teens	Young Adults	Over 30	Senior Citizens
★★★½	★★★½	★★★½	★★★½	★★★½	★★★½

DESCRIPTION AND COMMENTS   A very elaborate shooting gallery which costs fifty cents to play. One of the few attractions in Disneyland not included in the admission pass.

TOURING TIPS   Good fun for them what likes to shoot, but definitely not a place to blow time if you are on a tight schedule. Try it on your second day if time allows.

Mike Fink Keelboats

Type of Ride: Scenic boat ride

When to Go: Before 11 A.M.

Special Comments: Don't ride if the lines are long. Closes at dusk.

Authors' Rating: ★★★

Overall Appeal by Age Group:

Pre-school	Grade School	Teens	Young Adults	Over 30	Senior Citizens
★★★½	★★★	★★★	★★★	★★★	★★★

Duration of Ride: 10½ minutes

Average Wait in Line per 100 People Ahead of You: 19 minutes

Assumes: 2 boats operating

Loading Speed: Slow

DESCRIPTION AND COMMENTS   Small river keelboats which circle Tom Sawyer Island and Fort Wilderness, taking the same route as the Explorer Canoes, the Mark Twain Steamboat and the Sailing Ship Columbia. The top deck and the lower bow seats of the keelboat afford the best view but are exposed to the elements.

TOURING TIPS   This trip covers the same circle traveled by the Explorer Canoes, the Mark Twain Steamboat, and the Sailing Ship Columbia. Keelboats and the canoes load slowly so we usually prefer the larger craft. The other way to see much of the area covered by the respective boat tours is to explore Tom Sawyer Island and Fort Wilderness on foot.

Mark Twain Steamboat

Type of Ride: Scenic boat ride

When to Go: Between 11 A.M. and 5 P.M.

Special Comments: Suspends operation at dusk

Authors' Rating: Provides an excellent vantage point; ★★★

Overall Appeal by Age Group:

Pre-school	Grade School	Teens	Young Adults	Over 30	Senior Citizens
★★★	★★★	★★½	★★★	★★★	★★★

Duration of Ride: About 14 minutes

Average Wait to Board: 10 minutes

Assumes: Normal operations

Loading Method: En masse

DESCRIPTION AND COMMENTS   Large capacity paddle wheel riverboat which navigates the waters around Tom Sawyer Island and Fort Wilderness. A beautiful craft, the Steamboat provides a lofty perch from which to see Frontierland and New Orleans Square.

TOURING TIPS   One of four boat rides that survey the same real estate. Since the Explorer Canoes and the Mike Fink Keelboats are slower loading, we think the Steamboat (along with the Sailing Ship Columbia, which is also large and loads at the same landing) makes more efficient use of touring time. If you are not in the mood for a boat ride, much of the same sights can be seen by hiking around Tom Sawyer Island and Fort Wilderness.

Sailing Ship Columbia

Type of Ride: Scenic boat ride

When to Go: Between 11 A.M. and 5 P.M.

Special Comments: Suspends operation at dusk

Sailing Ship Columbia (continued)

Authors' Rating: A stunning piece of workmanship; ★★★★
Overall Appeal by Age Group:

Pre-school	Grade School	Teens	Young Adults	Over 30	Senior Citizens
★★★★	★★★★	★★★	★★★½	★★★★	★★★★

Duration of Ride: About 14 minutes
Average Wait to Board: 10 minutes
Assumes: Normal operations
Loading Method: En masse

DESCRIPTION AND COMMENTS   The Columbia is a stunning replica of a three-masted 18th-century merchant ship. Both above and below decks are open to visitors with below decks outfitted to depict the life and work environment of the ship's crew in 1787. The Columbia operates only on busier days and runs the same route as the canoes, keelboats, and the Mark Twain Steamboat. As with the other river craft, the Columbia suspends operations at dusk.

TOURING TIPS   The Columbia, along with the Mark Twain Steamboat, provides a short-wait, high-carrying-capacity alternative for cruising the Rivers of America. We found the Columbia beautiful in her craftsmanship and by far the most aesthetically pleasing and historically interesting of any of the four choices of boat rides on the Rivers of America.

If you have time to be choosy, ride aboard the Columbia. After boarding, while waiting for the cruise to begin, tour below deck. Once under way, come topside and stroll the deck, taking in the beauty and complexity of the rigging.

The Columbia does not usually require a long wait, making it a good bet during the crowded afternoon hours.

—— *Frontierland Eateries and Shops* ——

DESCRIPTION AND COMMENTS   More specialty and souvenir shopping and undistinguished bulk food for the masses.

TOURING TIPS   Don't waste time browsing in shops or standing in line for food unless you have a very relaxed schedule or came specifically to shop.

Fantasyland

Truly an enchanting place, spread gracefully like a miniature Alpine Village beneath the towers of Sleeping Beauty Castle, Fantasyland is the heart of the park. Renovated and upgraded in 1983, the Fantasyland attractions became the happy beneficiaries of a new generation of Disney technology and special effects.

Sleeping Beauty Castle

Type of Attraction: Walk-through exhibit
When to Go: Before 11 A.M. and after 5 P.M.
Special Comments: Entrance is just through the Castle gate to the left.
Authors' Rating: Very pleasant when not congested; ★★★½
Overall Appeal by Age Group:

Pre-school	Grade School	Teens	Young Adults	Over 30	Senior Citizens
★★★	★★★	★★	★★★	★★★	★★★

DESCRIPTION AND COMMENTS Unnoticed by many, a rather small, unobtrusive sign marks the entrance to Sleeping Beauty Castle. Stepping inside, the visitor moves through the interior of the Castle via a convoluted narrow passage. Situated at intervals along the passage are dioramas depicting the story of Sleeping Beauty.

TOURING TIPS A pleasant change of pace for adults and a sort of adventure for kids. Animatronics enliven the diorama scenes as Sleeping Beauty's story unfolds.

On the negative side, the passageway is small and winding. Once inside you are trapped and must move at the pace of those in front of you (which on a busy day is very slow indeed). If you are in a hurry or suffer claustrophobia, don't try the Castle during the 11 A.M. to 5 P.M. period.

It's a Small World

Type of Ride: Scenic boat ride
When to Go: Anytime except after a parade
Authors' Rating: A delightful change of pace; ★★★★
Overall Appeal by Age Group:

Pre-school	Grade School	Teens	Young Adults	Over 30	Senior Citizens
★★★★	★★★½	★★★	★★★★	★★★★	★★★★

Duration of Ride: 11–14 minutes
Average Wait in Line per 100 People Ahead of You: 2½ minutes
Assumes: Busy conditions with 56 boats operating
Loading Speed: Fast

DESCRIPTION AND COMMENTS   A happy, upbeat attraction with a world brotherhood theme and a catchy tune that will roll around in your head for weeks. Small boats convey visitors on a tour around the world, with singing and dancing dolls showcasing the dress and culture of each nation. Almost everyone enjoys It's a Small World, but it stands, along with the Enchanted Tiki Room, as an attraction that some could take or leave while others think it is one of the real masterpieces of Disneyland. We rank it as a "not to be missed" attraction. Try it and form your own opinion.

TOURING TIPS   A "not to be missed" attraction, It's a Small World is a fast loading ride that is usually a good bet during the busier times of the day. The boats are moved along by water pressure, with the pressure increased by adding boats. Thus the more boats in service when you ride (up to a maximum total of 60) the shorter the duration of the ride (and wait).

Skyway to Tomorrowland

Type of Ride: Scenic transportation to Tomorrowland
When to Go: Before 11:30 A.M. and after 5 P.M.
Special Comments: If there is a line, it's probably quicker to walk.
Authors' Rating: Nice view; ★★★★

Skyway to Tomorrowland (*continued*)

Overall Appeal by Age Group:

Pre-school	Grade School	Teens	Young Adults	Over 30	Senior Citizens
★★★★	★★★★	★★★½	★★★½	★★★½	★★★½

Duration of Ride: Approximately 4 minutes one way

Average Wait in Line per 100 People Ahead of You: 9 minutes

Assumes: 42 cars operating

Loading Speed: Moderate

DESCRIPTION AND COMMENTS   Part of the Disneyland internal transportation system, the Skyway is a chair lift which conveys patrons high above the park to Tomorrowland. The view is great, and sometimes the Skyway can even save a little shoe leather, but it's usually faster to walk.

TOURING TIPS   We enjoy this scenic trip early in the morning, during the afternoon Character Parade, during an evening parade, or just before closing. In short, before the crowds fill the park, when they are otherwise occupied, or when they are on the decline. These times also provide the most dramatic and beautiful vistas.

Peter Pan's Flight

Type of Ride: A Disney fantasy adventure

When to Go: Before 11 A.M.

Authors' Rating: Happy, mellow, and well done; ★★★★

Overall Appeal by Age Group:

Pre-school	Grade School	Teens	Young Adults	Over 30	Senior Citizens
★★★★	★★★★	★★★½	★★★★	★★★★	★★★★

Duration of Ride: 2⅓ minutes

Average Wait in Line per 100 People Ahead of You: 11 minutes

Assumes: 13 ships operating

Loading Speed: Slow

DESCRIPTION AND COMMENTS   Though not considered to be one of the major attractions, Peter Pan's Flight is superbly designed and

Peter Pan's Flight (*continued*)

absolutely delightful, with a happy theme, a reunion with some un-forgettable Disney characters, beautiful effects and charming music.

TOURING TIPS   Though not a major feature of Disneyland, we never-theless classify it as "not to be missed." Try to ride before 11 A.M. or after 5 P.M., or during the afternoon Character Parade.

King Arthur Carousel

Type of Ride: Merry-go-round
When to Go: Before 11:30 A.M. or after 5 P.M.
Special Comments: Adults enjoy the beauty and nostalgia of this ride.
Authors' Rating: A beautiful children's ride; ★★★
Overall Appeal by Age Group:

Pre-school	Grade School	Teens	Young Adults	Over 30	Senior Citizens
★★★★	★★½	★	★★½	★★★	★★★

Duration of Ride: A little over 2 minutes
Average Wait in Line per 100 People Ahead of You: 8 minutes
Assumes: Normal staffing
Loading Speed: Slow

DESCRIPTION AND COMMENTS   A merry-go-round to be sure, but cer-tainly one of the most elaborate and beautiful you will ever see, espe-cially when lighted at night.

TOURING TIPS   Unless there are small children in your party, we sug-gest you appreciate this ride from the sidelines. If your children insist on riding, try to get them on before 11:30 A.M. or after 5 P.M. While nice to look at, the Carousel loads and unloads very slowly.

Mr. Toad's Wild Ride

Type of Ride: Disney version of a spook-house track ride
When to Go: Before 11 A.M.
Authors' Rating: Much improved; ★★★

Mr. Toad's Wild Ride (*continued*)

Overall Appeal by Age Group:

Pre-school	Grade School	Teens	Young Adults	Over 30	Senior Citizens
★★★½	★★★½	★★★½	★★★	★★★	★★★

Duration of Ride: Almost 2 minutes

Average Wait in Line per 100 People Ahead of You: 9 minutes

Assumes: 12 cars operating

Loading Speed: Slow to moderate

DESCRIPTION AND COMMENTS This is perhaps the ride that profited most by the Fantasyland renovation. Refurbished with some fun special effects, the ride finally comes close to living up to the allure of its name.

TOURING TIPS Not a great but certainly a good attraction (and a very popular one). Lines build early in the day and never let up. Catch Mr. Toad before 11 A.M.

Snow White's Scary Adventures

Type of Ride: Disney version of spook-house track ride

When to Go: Before 11 A.M. and after 5 P.M.

Special Comments: Not really very scary

Authors' Rating: Worth seeing if the wait is not long; ★★★

Overall Appeal by Age Group:

Pre-school	Grade School	Teens	Young Adults	Over 30	Senior Citizens
★★★	★★★	★★½	★★★	★★★	★★★

Duration of Ride: Almost 2 minutes

Average Wait in Line per 100 People Ahead of You: 9 minutes

Assumes: 10 cars operating

Loading Speed: Moderate

DESCRIPTIONS AND COMMENTS Here you ride in a mining car through a spook house with a Perils-of-Pauline flavor, starring Snow White as she narrowly escapes harm at the hands of the wicked witch. The action and effects are a cut above Mr. Toad's Wild Ride but not as good as Peter Pan's Flight.

Snow White's Scary Adventures (continued)

TOURING TIPS   Enjoyable but not particularly compelling. Experience it if the lines are not too long or on a second-day visit. Ride before noon or after 5:00 if possible. Also, don't take the "Scary" part too seriously. The witch looks mean, but most kids take her in stride.

Alice in Wonderland

Type of Ride: Disney version of a spook-house track ride
When to Go: Before 11 A.M. or after 5 P.M.
Special Comments: Do not confuse with Mad Tea Party ride.
Authors' Rating: Great characterization and story line; ★★★½
Overall Appeal by Age Group:

Pre-school	Grade School	Teens	Young Adults	Over 30	Senior Citizens
★★★½	★★★½	★★★½	★★★½	★★★½	★★★½

Duration of Ride: Almost 4 minutes
Average Wait in Line per 100 People Ahead of You: 9 minutes
Assumes: 16 cars operating
Loading Speed: Moderate

DESCRIPTION AND COMMENTS   A newer ride with some nice surprises and special effects, which tells the story of Alice in Wonderland. Guests ride in nifty caterpillar cars in a winding, spook-house environment.

TOURING TIPS   This is a very well done ride in the best Disney tradition; familiar characters, good effects, and a theme that you can follow. Ride before 11 A.M. or after 5 P.M.

Pinocchio's Daring Journey

Type of Ride: Disney version of a spook-house track ride
When to Go: Before 11:30 A.M. and after 4:30 P.M.
Authors' Rating: A big letdown; ★★½
Overall Appeal by Age Group:

Pre-school	Grade School	Teens	Young Adults	Over 30	Senior Citizens
★★★	★★★	★★½	★★½	★★½	★★½

Pinocchio's Daring Journey (*continued*)

Duration of Ride: Almost 3 minutes
Average Wait in Line per 100 People Ahead of You: 8 minutes
Assumes: 15 cars operating
Loading Speed: Moderate

DESCRIPTION AND COMMENTS   Another enclosed, spook-house-genre ride that traces the adventures of Pinocchio as he tries to find his way home.

TOURING TIPS   One of the newer Fantasyland rides, Pinocchio doesn't quite live up to expectations. The action is difficult to follow and lacks continuity. The special effects are O.K.—just O.K. The word must be out on Pinocchio because the lines are seldom very long. Still, the best time to ride is before 11:30 A.M. and after 4:30 P.M.

Matterhorn Bobsleds

Type of Ride: Roller coaster
When to Go: Right after the park opens and during the hour before it closes.
Special Comments: Children must be 3′4″ tall to ride. Children under 7 years must ride with an adult.
Authors' Rating: Fun ride but not too scary; ★★★½
Overall Appeal by Age Group:

Pre-school	Grade School	Teens	Young Adults	Over 30	Senior Citizens
†	★★★★	★★★★	★★★★	★★★★	★★★★

†Some preschoolers loved Matterhorn Bobsleds; others were frightened.

Duration of Ride: 2⅓ minutes
Average Wait in Line per 100 People Ahead of You: 13 minutes
Assumes: Both tracks operating with 10 sleds per track, 23-second dispatch intervals
Loading Speed: Moderate

DESCRIPTION AND COMMENTS   The Matterhorn is the most distinctive landmark on the Disneyland scene, visible from almost anywhere in

Matterhorn Bobsleds (*continued*)

the park. A venerable old ride, and one of the few thrill rides in the Disney repertoire, the Matterhorn maintains its popularity and long lines year in and year out. The Matterhorn Bobsleds is a roller coaster ride with an Alpine motif. On the scary scale, the ride ranks about 7 on a scale of 10 (about the same as Space Mountain). The special effects cannot compare to Space Mountain, but do afford a few nifty surprises.

TOURING TIPS   Lines for the Matterhorn form as soon as the gates open and persist throughout the day. Ride first thing in the morning or just before the park closes. If you are a roller coaster person, ride Space Mountain and then hurry over and hop on the Matterhorn first thing in the morning. If roller coasters are not the end-all for you, we recommend choosing one or the other of the roller coasters, or saving one for a second day.

Casey Jr. Circus Train

Type of Ride: Miniature train

When to Go: Before 11 A.M. and after 5 P.M.

Authors' Rating: A quiet scenic ride; ★★★

Overall Appeal by Age Group:

Pre-school	Grade School	Teens	Young Adults	Over 30	Senior Citizens
★★★★	★★★	★½	★★★	★★★	★★★

Duration of Ride: A little over 3 minutes

Average Wait in Line per 100 People Ahead of You: 12 minutes

Assumes: Two trains operating

Loading Speed: Slow

DESCRIPTION AND COMMENTS   A long-standing attraction and a pet project of Walt Disney, Casey Jr. circulates through a landscape of miniature towns, farms, and lakes.

TOURING TIPS   This ride covers the same sights as the Storybook Land Canal Boats, but does it faster and with less of a wait. Accommodations for adults, however, are less than optimal on this ride, with some passengers having to squeeze into diminutive caged cars (after all, it is a circus train).

Storybook Land Canal Boats

Type of Ride: Scenic boat ride
When to Go: Before 10:30 A.M. and after 5:30 P.M.
Authors' Rating: Pretty, tranquil, and serene; ★★★★
Overall Appeal by Age Group:

Pre-school	Grade School	Teens	Young Adults	Over 30	Senior Citizens
★★★	★★½	★★½	★★★½	★★★½	★★★½

Duration of Ride: 9½ minutes
Average Wait in Line per 100 People Ahead of You: 16 minutes
Assumes: 7 boats operating
Loading Speed: Slow

DESCRIPTION AND COMMENTS   Guide-operated boats wind along canals situated beneath the same miniature landscapes visible from the Casey Jr. Circus Train.

TOURING TIPS   The boats are much more comfortable than the train, the view of the miniatures is better, and the pace is more leisurely. On the down side the lines are long, and if not long, definitely slow-moving, and the ride itself takes a lot of time. Our recommendation is to ride Casey Jr. if you only have one day and to take the boat if you have two days. If you ride the Canal Boats, try to get on before 10 A.M.

Dumbo the Flying Elephant

Type of Ride: Disneyfied midway ride
When to Go: Before 10:30 A.M. and during the late evening
Authors' Rating: An attractive children's ride: ★★★½
Overall Appeal by Age Group:

Pre-school	Grade School	Teens	Young Adults	Over 30	Senior Citizens
★★★★	★★★	★★	★½	★½	★½

Duration of Ride: 1⅔ minutes
Average Wait in Line per 100 People Ahead of You: 18 minutes
Assumes: Normal staffing
Loading Speed: Slow

Dumbo the Flying Elephant (continued)

DESCRIPTION AND COMMENTS A nice, tame, happy children's ride based on the lovable Disney flying elephant character. An upgraded rendition of a ride that can be found at state fairs and amusement parks across the country.

TOURING TIPS This is a slow-load ride that we recommend you bypass unless you are on a very relaxed touring schedule. If your kids are excited about Dumbo, try to get them on the ride before 10:30 A.M. or try just before the park closes.

Mad Tea Party

Type of Ride: Midway type spinning ride

When to Go: Before 11 A.M. and after 5 P.M.

Special Comments: You can make the teacups spin faster by turning the wheel in the center of the cup.

Authors' Rating: Fun but not worth the wait; ★★

Overall Appeal by Age Group:

Pre-school	Grade School	Teens	Young Adults	Over 30	Senior Citizens
★★★½	★★★½	★★★½	★★½	★★	★★

Duration of Ride: 1½ minutes

Average Wait in Line per 100 People Ahead of You: 8 minutes

Assumes: Normal staffing

Loading Speed: Slow

DESCRIPTION AND COMMENTS Well done in the Disney style, but still just an amusement park ride. The Alice in Wonderland Mad Hatter provides the theme and patrons whirl around feverishly in big teacups. A rendition of this ride, sans Disney characters, can be found at every local carnival and fair.

TOURING TIPS This ride, aside from not being particularly unique, is notoriously slow loading. Skip it on a busy schedule if the kids will let you. Ride in the morning of your second day if your schedule is more relaxed.

Fantasyland Autopia

Type of Ride: Drive 'em yourself miniature cars
When to Go: Before 10 A.M. and after 5 P.M.
Special Comments: Must be 4′4″ tall to drive. Only open on busy days.
Authors' Rating: Boring; ★
Overall Appeal by Age Group:

Pre-school	Grade School	Teens	Young Adults	Over 30	Senior Citizens
★★★½	★★★	★	½	½	½

Duration of Ride: Approximately 4½ minutes
Average Wait in Line per 100 People Ahead of You: 6 minutes
Assumes: 35 cars operating on each track
Loading Speed: Slow

DESCRIPTION AND COMMENTS A close copy of the Tomorrowland Autopia. Only open on busier days, the Autopia consists of a winding miniature freeway where you can drive a one-cylinder convertible at speeds of up to seven miles an hour. All vehicles run on a track so there is no passing. Children must be at least four feet, four inches tall to drive, or be accompanied by an adult. With the scenery as dull as the ride, most visitors over the age of ten chalk up the Autopia as a big yawn.

TOURING TIPS This ride is an anachronism in the age of modern Disney technology. We suggest you skip it entirely unless you have small children in your party. If you ride, go before 11 A.M. or after 5 P.M.

Motor Boat Cruise

Type of Ride: Sedate cruise in a miniature motor boat
When to Go: Before 11 A.M. or after 5 P.M.
Special Comments: Skip this unless you have small children.
Authors' Rating: Boring; ★★
Overall Appeal by Age Group:

Pre-school	Grade School	Teens	Young Adults	Over 30	Senior Citizens
★★★★	★★½	★½	★½	★★	★★½

Motor Boat Cruise (continued)

Duration of Ride: 4½ minutes
Average Wait in Line per 100 People Ahead of You: 7 minutes
Assumes: Both channels operating with 20 or 21 boats per channel
Loading Speed: Slow

DESCRIPTION AND COMMENTS   The wet version of the Fantasyland Autopia, patrons drive small motorboats through a convoluted system of waterways. Once again it's slow-go, single file, with not much to see along the way. Children under four feet, four inches tall must be accompanied by an adult.

TOURING TIPS   Loading is slow and lines are often long for this less-than-inspiring ride. Small children enjoy the Motor Boat Cruise, but for many other visitors it's a bore and a waste of time. We suggest that you bypass this one or ride before 11 A.M. or after 5 P.M.

Videopolis

DESCRIPTION AND COMMENTS   This is modern Disney management's accommodation to teens. Open evenings, the Videopolis is a spectacular teen nightclub featuring a combination of live music, rock videos, special effects, and dancing on a 5,000-square-foot dance floor.

TOURING TIPS   Rock and Roll is here to stay, finally. A great hangout for teens and for young-at-heart older folks.

—— Fantasyland Eateries and Shops ——

DESCRIPTION AND COMMENTS   It's no big secret that we find the food in Disneyland edible but certainly mediocre. Fantasyland food is no exception. In Fantasyland, the fare, in addition to being bland, is also in short supply. Only the modest Village Haus Restaurant serves Fantasyland's teeming masses.

TOURING TIPS   Fast food is anything but in Fantasyland, and shopping is ho-hum, with the possible exception of Mickey's Christmas Chalet, a shop which specializes in Christmas decor year round. Don't waste time on the shops unless you have a relaxed schedule or unless shopping is a big priority.

Tomorrowland

Tomorrowland is a futuristic mix of rides and experiences which relates to the technological development of man and what life will be like in the years to come. If this sounds a little bit like the EPCOT Center theme, it's because it is. Tomorrowland was very much a breeding ground for the ideas which resulted in EPCOT Center. Yet Tomorrowland and EPCOT Center are very different. Aside from differences in scale, Tomorrowland is more "just for fun." While EPCOT Center educates in its own delightful style, Tomorrowland allows you to hop in and try the future on for size.

Star Tours

Type of Attraction: Space flight simulation ride
When to Go: Before 10 A.M.
Special Comments: Expectant mothers are advised against riding
Authors' Rating: A blast; not to be missed; ★★★★★
Overall Appeal by Age Group:

Pre-school	Grade School	Teens	Young Adults	Over 30	Senior Citizens
★★★★★	★★★★★	★★★★★	★★★★★	★★★★★	★★★★★

Duration of Ride: Approximately 7 minutes
Average Wait in Line per 100 People Ahead of You: 5 minutes
Assumes: 4 simulators operating
Loading Speed: Moderate

DESCRIPTION AND COMMENTS   This newest Disneyland attraction consists of a ride in a flight simulator modeled after those used in the training of pilots and astronauts. Guests watch the scenery flash by at supersonic speed while the simulator bucks and pitches for added effect. A first-class addition to the Disney adventure ride repertoire.

TOURING TIPS   This ride will be the Disneyland headliner for some months to come and can be counted on to draw large crowds throughout the day. Ride first thing in the morning or just before the park closes.

Space Mountain

Type of Ride: Roller coaster in the dark

When to Go: First thing when the park opens or during the hour before closing or between 6 and 7 P.M.

Special Comments: Not all that wild if you are a roller coaster lover

Authors' Rating: Good roller coaster with excellent special effects; ★★★★

Overall Appeal by Age Group:

Pre-school	Grade School	Teens	Young Adults	Over 30	Senior Citizens
†	★★★★★	★★★★★	★★★★	★★★★	†

†Children must be 3′4″ tall to ride. Some preschoolers loved Space Mountain, others were frightened. The sample size of senior citizens who experienced this ride was too small to develop an accurate rating.

Duration of Ride: 2¾ minutes

Average Wait in Line per 100 People Ahead of You: 3½ minutes

Assumes: 11 cars operating at 20-second dispatch intervals

Loading Speed: Moderate to fast

DESCRIPTION AND COMMENTS   Space Mountain is a roller coaster in the dark. Totally enclosed in a mammoth futuristic structure, the attraction is a marvel of creativity and engineering. The theme of the ride is a space flight through the dark recesses of the galaxy. The effects are superb and the ride is the fastest and wildest in the Disney repertoire. As a roller coaster, Space Mountain is on a par with the Matterhorn Bobsleds, but with much better special effects, and it's much zippier than the rather tame Big Thunder Mountain Railroad.

TOURING TIPS   Space Mountain is a "not to be missed" feature (if you can handle a fairly wild roller coaster ride). People who are not timid about going on roller coasters will take Space Mountain in stride. What sets Space Mountain apart is that the cars plummet through the dark with only occasional lighting effects piercing the gloom. Try to ride Space Mountain before 9:30 A.M., during the hour before the park closes, or between 6 and 7 P.M.

Submarine Voyage

Type of Ride: Adventure/scenic boat ride
When to Go: Before 10 A.M. or during the hour before the park closes
Authors' Rating: Interesting and fun; ★★★★
Overall Appeal by Age Group:

Pre-school	Grade School	Teens	Young Adults	Over 30	Senior Citizens
★★★★	★★★★	★★★	★★★½	★★★½	★★★★

Duration of Ride: Approximately 10 minutes
Average Wait in Line per 100 People Ahead of You: 5 minutes
Assumes: 8 submarines operating
Loading Speed: Slow to moderate

DESCRIPTION AND COMMENTS   This attraction is equipped with modern submarines, in contrast to the Captain Nemo models used at Walt Disney world in Florida. Otherwise, the rides are almost identical, consisting of a submarine voyage which encounters mermaids, sea serpents, a variety of marine life (robotic), sunken ships, giant squids, and other sights and adventures. It struggles to maintain its image along with such marvels as Pirates of the Caribbean or Space Mountain. All things considered, though, it's still a darn nifty experience and one which we put in our "not to be missed" category.

TOURING TIPS   This is a slow-loading, moderate-capacity ride. To avoid long lines, ride before 10 A.M. or right before the park closes. Note that we do list the Submarine Voyage as a "not to be missed" attraction.

Tomorrowland Autopia

Type of Ride: Drive-'em-yourself miniature cars
When to Go: Before 10 A.M. and after 5 P.M.
Special Comments: Must be 4'4" tall to drive
Authors' Rating: Boring; ★

Tomorrowland Autopia (*continued*)

Overall Appeal by Age Group:

Pre-school	Grade School	Teens	Young Adults	Over 30	Senior Citizens
★★★½	★★★	★	½	½	½

Duration of Ride: Approximately 4½ minutes
Average Wait in Line per 100 People Ahead of You: 6 minutes
Assumes: 35 cars operating on each track
Loading Speed: Slow

DESCRIPTION AND COMMENTS   An elaborate miniature freeway with gasoline-powered cars that will travel at speeds of up to seven miles an hour. The raceway design, with its sleek cars, auto race noises, and highway signs, is quite alluring. In fact, however, the cars poke along on a track leaving the driver with little to do. Pretty ho hum for most adults and teenagers. Of those children who would enjoy the ride, many are excluded by the requirement that drivers be 4'4" tall. The ride is almost identical to the Fantasyland Autopia except the scenery is marginally better, with more ramps and overpasses.

TOURING TIPS   This ride is appealing to the eye but definitely expendable to the schedule. Try it your second day if the kids are reluctant to omit it. Ride before 10 A.M. or after 5 P.M.

Skyway to Fantasyland

Type of Ride: Scenic transportation to Fantasyland
When to Go: Before 11 A.M. and after 5 P.M.
Special Comments: If there is a line, it's probably quicker to walk.
Authors' Rating: Nice view; ★★★½
Overall Appeal by Age Group:

Pre-school	Grade School	Teens	Young Adults	Over 30	Senior Citizens
★★★★	★★★★	★★★½	★★★½	★★★½	★★★½

Duration of Ride: Approximately 4 minutes one way
Average Wait in Line per 100 People Ahead of You: 9 minutes
Assumes: 42 cars operating
Loading Speed: Moderate

DESCRIPTION AND COMMENTS   A skylift which will transport you from Tomorrowland to the far corner of Fantasyland near the border it shares with Frontierland. The view is one of the best in Disneyland, but walking is usually faster if you just want to get there.

TOURING TIPS   Unless the lines are short, the Skyway will not save you any time as a mode of transportation. As a ride, however, it affords some incredible views. Ride early in the morning, during the two hours before the park closes, or during one of the daily parades, which tend to siphon the crowds from the rides.

Rocket Jets

Type of Ride: Very mild midway-type thrill ride
When to Go: Before 10 A.M. or during the hour before the park closes
Authors' Rating: Not worth the wait; ★
Overall Appeal by Age Group:

Pre-school	Grade School	Teens	Young Adults	Over 30	Senior Citizens
★★★★	★★★½	★★★	★★	★	★

Duration of Ride: 1½ minutes
Average Wait in Line per 100 People Ahead of You: 13 minutes
Assumes: Normal staffing
Loading Speed: Slow

DESCRIPTION AND COMMENTS   A carnival-type ride involving small rockets which rotate on arms around a central axis.

TOURING TIPS   Slow loading and expendable on any schedule.

PeopleMover

Type of Ride: Scenic
When to Go: During the hot, crowded period of the day (11:30 A.M.– 5 P.M.)
Special Comments: Loads under Rocket Jets platform via escalator
Authors' Rating: Scenic, relaxing, informative; ★★★½
Overall Appeal by Age Group:

Pre-school	Grade School	Teens	Young Adults	Over 30	Senior Citizens
★★★	★★★	★★½	★★★	★★★½	★★★½

PeopleMover (*continued*)

Duration of Ride: 12 minutes
Average Wait in Line per 100 People Ahead of You: 3½ minutes
Assumes: 34 trains operating
Loading Speed: Fast

DESCRIPTION AND COMMENTS   A unique prototype of a linear induction powered system of mass transportation. Tramlike cars take you on a leisurely tour of Tomorrowland, including a peek at the inside of Space Mountain.

TOURING TIPS   A nice, pleasant, relaxing ride, where the lines move quickly and are seldom long. A good ride to take during the busier times of the day.

Starcade

DESCRIPTION AND COMMENTS   Starcade is nothing more or less than a large (200-plus games) electronic games arcade.

TOURING TIPS   Nothing here you can't see at home.

America Sings

Type of Attraction: AudioAnimatronic musical presentation
When to Go: During the hot, crowded period of the day (11:30 A.M.–5 P.M.)
Authors' Rating: Not to be missed; ★★★★★
Overall Appeal by Age Group:

Pre-school	Grade School	Teens	Young Adults	Over 30	Senior Citizens
★★★★★	★★★★★	★★★★★	★★★★★	★★★★★	★★★★★

Duration of Presentation: About 20 minutes
Pre-Show Entertainment: None
Probable Waiting Time: Less than ten minutes

DESCRIPTION AND COMMENTS   *America Sings* is a happy, delightful journey through the history of American popular music, hosted and performed by an outrageous ensemble of AudioAnimatronic animals. From Stephen Foster to modern rock, it's all there, all upbeat, and all

American. We rank it as one of the better shows at Disneyland, and certainly a "not to be missed" attraction.

TOURING TIPS   Great music and great fun. Make sure you see this one. *America Sings* is a high-capacity theater attraction where the wait is never long. See the show during the heat of the day when a nice air-conditioned break from the crowds would be welcome.

Disneyland Railroad (for complete information, see same heading under Main Street)

DESCRIPTION AND COMMENTS   The Disneyland Railroad makes a regular stop at the Tomorrowland Railroad Station. For additional details about the Railroad see Disneyland Railroad in the Main Street write-up.

TOURING TIPS   This station becomes fairly crowded on busy days. If you are interested primarily in getting there, it may be quicker to walk.

Captain EO

Type of Attraction: 3-D rock 'n' roll space fantasy
When to Go: Summer and weekends: Before 11 A.M. and after 5 P.M.
     Off Season weekdays: Between noon and 5 P.M.
Special Comments: Do not miss.
Duration of Presentation: About 17 minutes
Pre-Show Entertainment: Video on how *Captain EO* was made
Probable Waiting Time: Varies with day of week and time of year

DESCRIPTION AND COMMENTS   *Captain EO* is sort of the ultimate rock video. Starring Michael Jackson as Captain EO, the film combines special theater effects (lasers, fiber optics, cannons, lights, etc.) with 3-D imagery, a host of memorable characters, rock music, and dance, to leave the audience yelling for more. The plot is flimsy but nobody seems to mind as *Captain EO*'s fast pace and upbeat delivery makes fans of teens and septuagenarians alike. Not to be missed.

TOURING TIPS   *Captain EO* draws huge crowds, especially on days when school is out and the crowd is younger. The theater, fortunately, is quite large (700-person capacity) so intimidating lines disappear quickly when a new audience is admitted. In our touring plans, we schedule *Captain EO* in the mid- to late afternoon and anticipate a bit

Captain EO (*continued*)

of a wait. This scheduling makes a lot of sense for someone who is trying to see as much as possible in one day. If, however, you are a repeat visitor, or are only interested in a select number of attractions, we recommend that you see *Captain EO* early in the morning after having experienced Star Tours and Space Mountain.

Mission to Mars

Type of Attraction: Simulated space trip

When to Go: During the hot, crowded period of the day (11:30 A.M.– 5 P.M.)

Special Comments: Special effects sometimes frighten toddlers.

Authors' Rating: Worthwhile; ★★★

Overall Appeal by Age Group:

Pre-school	Grade School	Teens	Young Adults	Over 30	Senior Citizens
★★	★★½	★★½	★★★	★★★	★★★

Duration of Presentation: About 10 minutes

Pre-Show Entertainment: About 6 minutes

Probable Waiting Time: Less than 10 minutes

DESCRIPTION AND COMMENTS   Actually a theater attraction, the show consists of a simulated flight from Earth to Mars. One of the oldest features of the park (originally called Flight to the Moon), Mission to Mars remains interesting and fun, with some surprising special effects.

TOURING TIPS   This show, while worthwhile, is not among the more popular attractions of the park. See Mission to Mars during the hot, crowded, middle part of the day.

Disneyland Monorail System

Type of Ride: Transportation/scenic

When to Go: During the hot, crowded period of the day (11:30 A.M.– 5 P.M.)

Special Comments: Take the Monorail to the Disneyland Hotel for lunch.

Authors' Rating: Nice relaxing ride with some interesting views of the park; ★★★

Disneyland Monorail System (*continued*)

Overall Appeal by Age Group:

Pre-school	Grade School	Teens	Young Adults	Over 30	Senior Citizens
★★★	★★★	★★★	★★★	★★★	★★★½

Duration of Ride: 12 minutes round trip
Average Wait in Line per 100 People Ahead of You: 10 minutes
Assumes: 3 monorails operating
Loading Speed: Moderate to fast

DESCRIPTION AND COMMENTS   The Monorail is a futuristic transportation ride which affords the only practical opportunity for escaping the park during the crowded lunch period and early afternoon. Boarding at the Tomorrowland Monorail Station, you can commute to the Disneyland Hotel complex where it's possible to have a nice lunch without fighting the crowds. For those not interested in lunch, the Monorail provides a tranquil round trip to the Hotel and back with a nice view of the parking lot and parts of Fantasyland and Tomorrowland.

TOURING TIPS   We recommend using the Monorail to commute to the Disneyland Hotel for a quiet relaxing lunch away from the crowds and the heat. If you only wish to experience the ride, go whenever you wish; the waits to board are seldom long.

World Premier Circle-Vision

Type of Attraction: Travel movie
When to Go: During the hot, crowded period of the day (11:30 A.M.–5 P.M.)
Special Comments: Audience must stand throughout presentation
Authors' Rating: Wonderful; not to be missed; ★★★★½
Overall Appeal by Age Group:

Pre-school	Grade School	Teens	Young Adults	Over 30	Senior Citizens
★★	★★★½	★★★★	★★★★½	★★★★★	★★★★★

Duration of Presentation: About 20 minutes
Pre-Show Entertainment: About 10 minutes
Probable Waiting Time: Less than ten minutes

World Premier Circle-Vision (*continued*)

DESCRIPTION AND COMMENTS   A theater attraction where visitors view an entertaining cartoon and film clip pre-show and are then ushered into the main theater to view the film *American Journeys*. The theater is unique in that the standing audience is completely surrounded by giant screens, which provide a 360-degree perspective of all the action in the movie. The film, an exceptionally well-done patriotic travelogue, features Colorado River rapids, glimpses of New Orleans and New York City, and spellbinding aerial photography of dozens of America's natural and man-made wonders. In addition to *American Journeys*, other Circle-Vision films, such as *Wonders of China* from the Chinese Pavilion at EPCOT Center, are sometimes shown.

TOURING TIPS   A high-capacity theater where the wait is seldom long. We suggest you visit during the hot, crowded afternoon hours.

—— *Tomorrowland Eateries* ——

DESCRIPTION AND COMMENTS   The Launching Pad and the Tomorrowland Terrace serve cold sandwiches. The Space Place is a good bet for short waits if you go early.

— Live Entertainment and Special Events at Disneyland —

Live entertainment in the form of bands, Disney character appearances, parades, singing and dancing, and ceremonies further enliven and add color to Disneyland on a daily basis. For specific information about what's going on the day you visit, stop by City Hall as you enter the park. Be forewarned, however, that if you are on a tight schedule, it is impossible to both see the park's featured attractions AND take in the numerous and varied live performances offered. In our One-Day Touring Plans we exclude the live performances in favor of seeing as much of the park as time permits. This is a considered tactical decision based on the fact that some of the parades and other performances siphon crowds away from the more popular rides, thus shortening waiting lines.

But the color and pageantry of live happenings around the park are an integral part of the Disneyland entertainment mix and a persuasive argument for second-day touring. The following is an incomplete list of those performances and events which are scheduled with some regularity and which require no reservations.

Disneyland Band	Disneyland's all-purpose band entertains around the park
Coke Corner Pianist	Piano favorites at the Coke Corner at the central-hub end of Main Street
Sax Quintet	A versatile quintet of saxes which plays on Main Street
Main Street Maniacs	A comic band featuring banjo, sax, and washboard, which plays on Main Street
Make Believe Brass	A big-sound brass group
Big Thunder Breakdown Boys	Bluegrass music in Bear Country and Frontierland
Royal Street Bachelors	A strolling Dixieland Band often seen in New Orleans Square

Mariachi Guadalajara	Traditional Latin-American music in front of the Casa Mexicana restaurant in Frontierland
Mountain Climbers	Real climbers scale the Matterhorn in Fantasyland
Krash & Airplay	Two high-energy Disney rock groups which perform at the Tomorrowland Terrace
Retreat Ceremony	Daily at around dusk in Town Square a small band and honor guard lower the flag and release a flock of white homing pigeons.
Parades	Parades begin near Small World in Fantasyland and proceed past Matterhorn Mountain to the central hub and then to the Town Square end of Main Street. Somedays the parades run the reverse route, starting on Main Street. Most parades feature some combination of marching bands, old-time vehicles, floats, and the Disney characters. On busier days special "theme" parades, which are even more spectacular than usual, are produced. Check with City Hall for the parade schedule.
	Main Street is the most crowded area from which to watch a parade, although the upper platform of the Main Street Train Station affords the best viewing perspective along the route. For less congested viewing try the Small World section of the parade route.
Fantasy in the Sky	A stellar fireworks display unleashed after dark on those nights the park is open until midnight
Tomorrowland Terrace Stage	The stage at Tomorrowland Terrace is the site of daily concerts, usually featuring the rock groups Krash and Airplay.
Disney Character Show (Fantasy Follies)	Song and dance stage shows featuring the Disney characters are performed at the Plaza Gardens on the central hub next to the Castle, according to a posted schedule.
Bands about Disneyland	Various banjo, dixieland, steel drum, marching, and fife and drum bands roam the park daily.

Walt Disney Character
Appearances

Walt Disney characters appear at random throughout the park but seemingly with more frequency in Fantasyland and on Main Street. Another good bet for character watching is at the Hungry Bear Restaurant in Bear Country.

Eating in Disneyland

Disneyland is a wonder and a marvel, a testimony to the creative genius of man. But for all of the beauty, imagination, and wholesomeness of this incredible place, it is almost impossible to obtain a decent meal. Simply put, what is available is food for the masses; bland, undistinguished, bulk. Logistically we are sympathetic; it is overwhelming to contemplate preparing and serving 100,000 or so meals each day. But our understanding, unfortunately, does not make the food any more palatable. Do not misconstrue, the food at Disneyland is not awful. It is merely mediocre in a place that has set the standard for virtually every other area of quality in tourism and entertainment. Given the challenge of feeding so many people each day, we might be more accepting of the banal fare if (1) we didn't believe the Disney people could do better, and if (2) obtaining food didn't require such an investment of time and effort. The variety found on the numerous menus indicates that somebody once had the right idea. Unfortunately, something was lost in the preparation, and what looks good on the printed menu loses its appeal when it appears on your plate.

Alternatives and Suggestions for Eating at Disneyland

1. Eat a good breakfast before arriving at Disneyland. You do not want to waste touring time eating breakfast at the park. Besides, there are some truly outstanding breakfast specials at restaurants outside of Disneyland.

2. Having eaten a good breakfast, keep your tummy happy as you tour by purchasing snacks from the vendors stationed throughout the park (or expressed differently: avoid restaurants!). This is especially important if you have a tight schedule; you cannot afford to spend a lot of time waiting in line for food.

3. If you are on a tight schedule and the park closes early, stay until closing and eat dinner outside of Disneyland before returning to your hotel. If the park stays open late, eat an early dinner at about 4 or 4:30 P.M. in the Disneyland eatery of your choice. You should have missed the last wave of lunch diners and sneaked in just ahead of the dinner crowd.

4. As an alternative to standing in line at Disneyland restaurants, try catching the Monorail at the Tomorrowland Monorail Station and commuting to the Disneyland Hotel Complex for lunch at one of its 16 restaurants and bars. The coming and going isn't nearly as time consuming as it appears, and you will probably be able to get a better meal, with faster service, in a more relaxed atmosphere. This option is recommended in our One- and Two-Day Touring Plans. The trip over and back takes very little time, and because most of the hotel guests have left for the park, the hotel restaurants are often slack.

5. If you are bound and determined to eat lunch in Disneyland, try to eat before 11:30 A.M. or after 2:30 P.M. The Hungry Bear Restaurant in Bear Country, the Casa Mexicana in Frontierland, the Tahitian Terrace in Adventureland, and the Space Place in Tomorrowland are good bets for shorter waiting if you go early. If you decide to eat your evening meal in the park, we recommend that you eat about 4:30 P.M., sneaking in just before the dinner rush. You will be able to eat after 8:30 P.M. (when the park is open late) without too much hassle, if you prefer. We recommend, however, that since there is a lot of super live entertainment beginning around 8 P.M., that you opt for an early meal. An excellent option, if it is convenient for you to be in New Orleans Square around 2 P.M., is to make a 6 P.M. reservation for dinner at the Blue Bayou. A 6 P.M. seating will assure that you will be done in time for the evening festivities. Also, the hour is early enough to preclude a backlog at the restaurant which would delay your being seated.

6. The Hungry Bear Restaurant in Bear Country, as well as the Launching Pad and the Tomorrowland Terrace in Tomorrowland, serve cold sandwiches of one sort or another. It is possible to buy a cold lunch (except for the drinks) before 11 A.M. and then carry your food until you are ready to eat. We met a family which does this routinely, with Mom always remembering to bring several small plastic bags for packing the food. Drinks can be purchased at the appropriate time from any convenient drink vendor.

7. Most fast-food eateries in Disneyland have more than one service window. Regardless of time of day, check out the lines at ALL of the windows before queuing up. Sometimes a manned (but out of the way) window will have a much shorter line or no line at all. Be forewarned that most patrons in the food lines are buying for their whole family or group, and that the ten people in line ahead of you will require the serving of thirty to forty, not just ten meals.

8. Sometimes cafeteria-style restaurants will move you through faster than the fast-food eateries. Since at the cafeterias it is customary for each family member to go through the line and select his own meal, you can get a better idea of how many persons must be served before you. Twenty-five persons ahead of you in a cafeteria line will usually signify a shorter wait than ten persons ahead of you in a fast-food line.

9. Don't expect quantum leaps in food quality from a sit-down, waitress-service restaurant. The atmosphere will be nicer, the prices higher, and the names of the entrees fancier, but the food will still be lackluster.

10. Restaurants which accept reservations for lunch and/or dinner fill their respective meal seatings quickly. The Blue Bayou in New Orleans Square takes reservations on busy days beginning about 2 P.M. The Golden Horseshoe in Frontierland operates almost exclusively by reservations, which should be made first thing in the morning. The Tahitian Terrace, which features the exotic and worthwhile *Polynesian Revue* dinner show, seats on a first-come, first-served basis. If you wish to attend any but the earliest show, line up at least an hour in advance.

11. For your general information, the Disney people have a park rule against bringing in your own food and drink. We interviewed one woman who, ignoring the rule, brought a huge picnic lunch for her family of five packed into a large diaper/baby paraphernalia bag. Upon entering the park she secured the bag in a locker at the Main Street guest locker facility to be retrieved later when the family was hungry. A San Diego family returned to their van in the parking lot for lunch. There they had a cooler, lawn chairs, and plenty of food, in the college football tailgating tradition.

Shopping in Disneyland

Shops in Disneyland add realism and atmosphere to the various theme settings and make available an extensive inventory of souvenirs, clothing, novelties, decorator items, and more. Much of the merchandise displayed (with the exception of Disney trademark souvenir items) is available back home and elsewhere at a lower price. In our opinion, shopping is not one of the main reasons for visiting Disneyland. We recommend bypassing the shops on a one-day visit. If you have two or more days to spend in Disneyland, browse the shops during the early afternoon when many of the attractions are crowded. Remember that Main Street—with its multitude of shops—opens one hour earlier and closes one hour later than the rest of the park. Lockers in the Main Street Train Station allow you to safely stash your purchases, saving the trouble of dragging them around the park with you.

PART FOUR—Touring Plans

Touring Plans: What They Are and How They Work

When we interviewed Disneyland visitors who toured the park on a slow day, say in early December, they invariably waxed eloquent about the sheer delight of their experience. When we questioned visitors, however, who toured on a moderate or busy day, they spent most of the interview telling us about the jostling crowds and how much time they stood in line. What a shame, they said, that you should devote so much time and energy to fighting the crowds in a place as special as Disneyland.

Given this complaint, we descended on Disneyland with a team of researchers to determine whether a touring plan could be devised that would move the visitor counter to the flow of the traffic and allow him to see virtually the whole park in one day with only minimal waits in line. On some of the busiest days of the year, our team monitored traffic flow into and through the park, noting how the park filled and how the patrons were distributed among the various lands. Likewise, we observed which rides and attractions were most popular and where bottlenecks were most likely to form.

After many long days of collecting data, we devised a number of preliminary touring plans which we tested during Easter week, one of the busiest weeks of the entire year. Each day individual members of our research team would tour the park according to one of the preliminary plans, noting how long it took to walk from place to place and how long the wait in line was for each ride or show. Combining the knowledge gained through these trial runs, we devised a master plan which we retested and fine-tuned. This plan, with very little variance from day to day, allowed us to experience all of the major rides and attractions, and most of the lesser ones, in one day, with an average in-line wait at each ride/show of less than five minutes.

From this master plan we developed a number of alternative plans which take into account the varying tastes and personal requirements of different Disneyland patrons. We devised a plan, for instance, for more mature guests that bypasses roller-coaster-type rides and requires less walking. Another plan was assembled for parents touring with children under the age of eight years. Each plan operates with the same efficiency as the master plan but addresses the special needs and preferences of its intended users.

Finally, after all of the plans were tested by our staff, we selected (using convenience sampling) a number of everyday Disneyland patrons to test the plans. The only prerequisite for being chosen for the test group (the visitors who would test the touring plans) was that the guest must be visiting a Disney attraction (including Walt Disney World) for the first time. A second group of ordinary Disneyland patrons was chosen for a "control group"—first-time visitors who would tour the park according to their own plans but who would make notes of what they did and how much time they spent waiting in lines.

When the two groups were compared, the results were no less than amazing. On days when the park's attendance exceeded 50,000, visitors touring on their own (without the plan) **averaged** 3.5 hours more waiting in line per day than the patrons touring according to our plan, and they experienced 31 percent fewer rides and attractions.

Will the Plans Continue to Work Once the Secret Is Out?   Yes!
First, all of the Plans require that a patron be on hand when Disneyland opens. Many vacationers simply refuse to make this early rising sacrifice, but you can see more in the one hour just after the park opens than in several hours once the park begins to fill. Second, it is anticipated that less than 1% of any given day's attendance will have been exposed to the Plans, not enough to bias the results. Last, most groups will interpret the Plans somewhat, skipping certain rides or shows as a matter of personal taste.

Variables That Will Affect the Success of the Touring Plans   How
quickly you move from one ride to another, when and how many refreshment and restroom breaks you take, when, where, and how you eat meals, and your ability (or lack thereof) to find your way around will all impact on the success of the Plans. We recommend continuous, expeditious touring until around 11:30 A.M. After that hour, breaks and so on will not effect the Plans significantly. If you are touring on a short-hours day (10 A.M.–6 P.M.) and the attendance is large, you may wish to avail yourself of one of the time-saving lunch options listed in the section "Eating in Disneyland."

General Overview   The Disneyland Touring Plans are step-by-step plans for seeing as much as possible in one day with a minimum of time wasted standing in line. They are designed to assist you in avoiding crowds and bottlenecks on days of moderate to heavy attendance. On days of lighter attendance (see "Selecting the Time of Year for Your Visit," page 14) the Plans will still save you time but will not be as critical to successful touring.

The Touring Plans

The One-Day Touring Plans are presented first, followed by a Two-Day Touring Plan. The first plan is presented in detail; not only do we provide you with an itinerary, but we also explain *why* we direct you as we do. Following the explanatory version of the Touring Plan for Adults (below), this Plan is recapped in outline form, which you can reproduce or tear out of the guide and take with you to the park. All of the other Touring Plans are presented in outline form only. The reasoning behind each of the other Plans is similar to that detailed in the explanatory version of the Touring Plan for Adults.

—— One-Day Touring Plan, for Adults (explanatory version) ——

FOR: **Adults touring with other adults, or adults touring with older children or teens.**

ASSUMES: Willingness to experience all major rides (including roller coasters) and shows.

GENERAL DIRECTIONS: On days of moderate to heavy attendance follow the Touring Plan exactly, deviating only when you do not wish to experience an attraction or ride called for on the Touring Plan. For instance, the Touring Plan may indicate that you go next to Tomorrowland and ride Space Mountain, a roller coaster ride. If you do not enjoy roller coasters, simply skip this step of the Plan and proceed to the next step.

SHORT-DAY TOURING: Sometimes Disneyland opens at 10 A.M. and closes at either 6 or 7 P.M. As a rule, lighter attendance on these days will compensate for the shortened visiting hours, and the Touring Plan will provide for efficient touring and short waits in line. If you are unlucky enough to encounter big crowds on a short-hours day, you may run out of time before you complete the Touring Plan. If you find

Disneyland packed on a day when the park closes early, follow the Touring Plan until the Plan calls for lunch. Then stop and scan the remainder of the Plan and scratch any rides or attractions which are of little or marginal interest to you. After lunch (or a snack if you don't wish to stop for lunch), follow the Touring Plan, but bypass the rides and shows that you crossed off. If you end up with some extra time before closing, hit one or two of the rides you eliminated earlier. If you are visiting Disneyland for the first time and are not sure which rides and shows should be on your "must see" list, see the section of this guide titled "Disneyland in Detail."

LONG LINES: Do not be alarmed if some of the lines seem long when you arrive as per the Touring Plan at a particular ride. The Plan is designed to minimize your waits, and even if a line appears long, trust us that it will move quickly. Over an entire day your waits will average about four to seven minutes per ride, but for two or three rides you may have to wait fifteen or twenty minutes (this will probably occur during the hour before lunch).

DIRECTION	EXPLANATION
1. Call (714) 999-4565 the day before your visit for the official opening time.	This will enable you to establish your early morning schedule. Be sure to eat a good breakfast before you go to the park.
2. Arrive an hour before the stated opening time. Main Street USA usually opens one hour before the park's official opening time, and the remainder of Disneyland usually opens a half hour before the official opening time. Purchase your admission and enter the park.	This will allow you to be one of the first patrons in the park, which will permit you to board many popular rides without long waits in line.
3. Do not stop on Main Street. Go directly to the central hub and wait until you are admitted to the rest of the park.	Main Street opens before the rest of Disneyland and consists primarily of shops and eateries. Since your objective is to beat the

DIRECTION	EXPLANATION
	crowds to the potential bottlenecks in the other areas of the park, you will postpone seeing Main Street until later when traffic there has dispersed and rides in other sections of the park have become crowded. Now you want to position yourself at the central hub so that you will be one of the first patrons to arrive at the first ride on the Touring Plan.
4. Turn right into Tomorrowland and ride Star Tours.	Star Tours is a new attraction that draws huge crowds as the park fills. If you do not ride first thing, you'll be in for a very long wait.
5. Go next door and ride Space Mountain.	This is an extremely popular ride that will have long lines almost all day. If you don't catch it first thing, you may have a wait of an hour or more to ride later in the day.
6. Go next to Fantasyland by way of Tomorrowland and ride the Matterhorn Bobsleds. If Space Mountain was enough roller coaster for a while, skip the Matterhorn and follow Step 6 Alternate. (We recommend skipping the Matterhorn Bobsleds unless you are really a roller coaster buff. The ride is very much like Space Mountain but the special effects are not as compelling.)	This is a very popular ride that loads at moderate speed. If you do not ride early in the morning you will have a long wait later. If you elect to skip the Matterhorn in favor of Step 6 Alternate, you will not have another opportunity to ride the Matterhorn without a long wait until twenty minutes before the park closes.

DIRECTION	EXPLANATION
6. ALTERNATE: While in Tomorrowland ride the Submarine Voyage.	Choosing this alternative will allow you more Disney variety while bypassing a thrill ride.
7. Go next to Fantasyland and ride Alice in Wonderland.	This is a newer ride and a slow loader. If you do not ride early in the morning you will have a long wait later.
8. While in Fantasyland ride Mr. Toad's Wild Ride.	This is a popular ride that loads very slowly. Lines grow very long at this ride as the day progresses.
9. While in Fantasyland ride Peter Pan's Flight.	Another popular ride and another slow loader. Waits for this ride become lengthy later in the day.
10. While in Fantasyland ride Snow White's Scary Adventures.	This ride is right across the walk from Peter Pan, making it convenient to enjoy at this time.
11. While in Fantasyland ride Pinocchio's Daring Journey.	This ride is right next door to Snow White, making it convenient to enjoy at this time.
12. Go to Adventureland via the Castle entrance and around the central hub and ride the Jungle Cruise.	This is a very popular, slow loading ride that is best enjoyed in the early morning.
13. Go next to New Orleans Square and ride Pirates of the Caribbean.	One of the most popular rides in the park, but one which can handle a lot of people efficiently. Do not worry if the line looks huge. It will move very quickly and the wait will not be bad.

NOTE: You will begin at this point to feel the effects of the crowd and your waits in line will increase somewhat. The next several rides may have

DIRECTION	EXPLANATION

lines which look intimidating compared to what you have experienced. But don't be concerned; these rides are well engineered and the lines will move fast.

14. While in New Orleans Square, experience the Haunted Mansion.	Another very popular ride. Once again, do not be dismayed by the size of the line; the wait will be short.
15. Go to Frontierland and ride the Big Thunder Mountain Railroad. We recommend in this Touring Plan that you catch the Monorail to the Disneyland Hotel for a nice lunch (see Step 19). If you are determined to eat in the park, eat after riding Big Thunder at the Casa Mexicana Restaurant directly opposite the entrance to the Big Thunder ride, or review other meal strategies in the "Eating in Disneyland" section of this guide.	Although this is another roller coaster ride, it is comparatively mild and more interesting for its special effects than as a wild ride. By the time you reach this ride it should be running at full capacity and your wait should be tolerable.

NOTE: This is about as far as you can go before the crowds catch up with you on a busy day, but you will have experienced many of the more popular rides and shows before the park filled up. On slower days you might be able to squeeze in one more major ride before the crunch hits. Note also that you are doing a considerable amount of walking. Don't be dismayed; this extra walking will literally save you as much as two hours of standing in line. But remember, during the early morning (up until 11 or 11:30 A.M.) do not dally between rides. With *Step 16* the Touring Plan shifts from the slower loading and/or extremely popular rides and shows (which need to be visited early in the day, before the park fills) to rides and shows which are engineered to handle large crowds effectively even at peak attendance.

16. While in Frontierland, take a cruise on the Rivers of America	Both boats load at the same landing. Take whichever arrives

DIRECTION	EXPLANATION
on either the Sailing Ship Columbia or the Mark Twain Steamboat.	first. The Columbia only operates on busy days.
17. Keeping Big Thunder Mountain on your right, take the path back to Fantasyland. Ride *either* the Casey Jr. Circus Train *or* the Storybook Land Canal Boats.	Both of these rides appear to be strictly for children, but are, in fact, delightful for persons of any age. Both rides traverse the same landscape, one on water and one on rails, so that there is really no need to ride both. On a busy day the wait will usually be shorter on the Casey Jr. Circus Train (the wait can sometimes be **very** long for the boats).
18. Keeping the Storybook Land Canal on your left, proceed across Fantasyland and ride It's a Small World.	It's a Small World is a popular mainstay of Disneyland and is engineered to move large numbers of people in a short time.
19. Keeping the Matterhorn on your right, proceed back to Tomorrowland and take the Monorail to the Disneyland Hotel complex for lunch. Have your hand stamped for reentry to the park when you get off the Monorail at the Hotel. If you have already eaten lunch, do not disembark at the hotel, but continue on the Monorail for a round trip.	Between 11:30 A.M. and 3:30 P.M. the lines at all of the restaurants in the park are ridiculous. At the same time, the numerous restaurants at the Disneyland Hotel complex can usually seat you with little or no waiting. In timed experiments, our staff enjoyed a leisurely lunch at one of the Disneyland Hotel eateries and returned to the park in not much more time than it took others of our colleagues to obtain burgers in one of the fast(?)-food lines. What many hungry people fail to recognize when they queue up at one of the park's fast-food diners is that almost every adult in line

DIRECTION	EXPLANATION
	ahead of them is buying not just for himself, but for his entire family or group. We have stood in these lines for up to five minutes without seeing one served customer emerge. Better to go to the hotel and take it easy. Plus you can eat in air conditioning and, if you wish, have an alcoholic beverage with your meal.
20. After lunch, return to the park on the Monorail.	You should feel rested following your lunch break.
21. After disembarking at the Tomorrowland Monorail Station take in a performance of *America Sings* (across from the Rocket Jets).	A large-capacity theater attraction with short waits almost no matter what the crowd.
22. Leaving *America Sings*, bear left and experience *Captain EO*.	You will probably have to wait a little here.
23. Exiting *Captain EO*, take in the *Mission to Mars*.	Another high-capacity theater that's a good bet in the heat of the afternoon.
24. Next ride the PeopleMover, accessible via escalator below the Rocket Jets platform.	Loads people in a hurry. Even if the line looks long your wait will be short.
25. Proceed to the World Premier Circle-Vision Theater on your right toward the main entrance of Tomorrowland.	Another short wait and a nice comfortable theater.
26. Depart Tomorrowland via its main entrance and go by way of the central hub back to Main	The Main Street Cinema is a fun, virtually ignored little spot which shows hilarious vintage silent

DIRECTION	EXPLANATION
Street. Stop at the Main Street Cinema for a few minutes.	movies and early Disney cartoons. Stay for 2 minutes or 20, according to your interest. There will not be a line.
27. Walk to the end of Main Street and turn left to *The Walt Disney Story* featuring *Great Moments with Mr. Lincoln.*	Once again, a cool, comfortable, high-capacity theater.
28. Next go to the Main Street Railroad Station and take the Disneyland Railroad around the park, **back past Main Street Station again** (don't get off) to the New Orleans Square Station (you will make $1\frac{1}{4}$ trips around the park).	On a crowded day Main Street Station is the easiest place to catch the train. Stay on **all the way around once, and then remain aboard** until you reach New Orleans Square Station for the second time.
29. Exit the Station and go left to Bear Country, walking past the Haunted Mansion with the river on your right. See the *Country Bear Jamboree.*	Two theaters showing the same presentation operate simultaneously here, keeping waiting to a minimum.
30. If the park is open late, the Hungry Bear Restaurant (next to *Country Bear Jamboree*) is a great spot to stop for a break. Sit well to the rear and you enjoy a delightful view of the various craft coming down the river. If the park closes early, you had better push on. There are still a few things to see.	Stop for a break here if time allows.
31. Exit Bear Country and pass the Haunted Mansion. Return to	This is a walk-through exhibit which you should be able to see

DIRECTION	EXPLANATION
New Orleans Square and from there go to Adventureland. Tour the Swiss Family Treehouse.	with little or no waiting at this time of day.
32. Exiting the Treehouse, go right to the Enchanted Tiki Room. See the show.	There could be a bit of a wait here, but probably not more than 20 minutes.
33. End of Touring Plan. If the park is open late, enjoy some of the evening parades and live entertainment, or do whatever you desire (including collapsing). If the park closes early remember that Main Street remains open a half hour to an hour after everything else shuts down.	Just before closing, the lines for all of the rides shrink drastically, allowing you to ride just about whatever you desire with little or no waiting. If you missed a ride or if a particular ride was not operating when you passed by earlier, the hour before closing is a good time to try again.

— Outline of One-Day Touring Plan, for Adults —

1. Call (714) 999-4565 the night before your visit to determine the "official" opening time.

2. Arrive at least one hour before the park opens. Buy your admission and enter the park.

3. Proceed directly to the end of Main Street and wait to be admitted to the rest of the park.

4. Turn right into Tomorrowland and ride Star Tours.

5. Exit to your right and ride Space Mountain.

6. Walk across Tomorrowland to Fantasyland and ride the Matterhorn Bobsleds. Or *instead*, while in Tomorrowland, ride the Submarine Voyage.

7. Go next to Fantasyland and ride Alice in Wonderland.

8. In Fantasyland, go around the corner toward the Castle and ride Mr. Toad's Wild Ride.

9. Go next door (toward the Castle) and ride Peter Pan's Flight.

10. Walk across the street and ride Snow White's Scary Adventures.

11. Go next door (away from the Castle) and ride Pinocchio's Daring Journey.

12. Exit Fantasyland through the Castle and proceed via the central hub to Adventureland. Ride the Jungle Cruise.

NOTE: The lines will begin to appear long and intimidating, but they will move quickly and your wait will be tolerable.

13. Turn left upon exiting the Jungle Cruise and go to New Orleans Square. Ride the Pirates of the Caribbean.

14. Turn left after exiting Pirates of the Caribbean and while in New Orleans Square experience the Haunted Mansion.

15. With the waterfront on your left, walk to Frontierland and ride Big Thunder Mountain Railroad.

DECISION TIME: We recommend eating lunch out of the park at the Disneyland Hotel complex (see Step 19). However, if you are resigned to eating in the park, we suggest that you eat after riding Big Thunder at the Casa Mexicana, across from the entrance to the Big Thunder Mountain Railroad.

16. Take the Mark Twain Steamboat or the Sailing Ship Columbia for a cruise of the Rivers of America.

17. Keeping Big Thunder Mountain on your right, take the path to Fantasyland and ride either the Casey Jr. Circus Train or the Storybook Land Canal Boats. If you stopped for lunch before arriving here, the lines may be prohibitive, in which case you should skip this step. Even a short line at the Canal Boats means a long wait.

18. Keeping the Storybook Land Canal on your left, proceed across Fantasyland and ride It's a Small World.

19. Walk back to Tomorrowland keeping the Matterhorn on your right and take the Monorail to the Disneyland Hotel complex for lunch. Have your hand stamped for reentry into the park when you disembark at the hotel. If you have already eaten stay aboard for a round trip.

20. After lunch, return to the park on the Monorail.

21. After disembarking at the Tomorrowland Monorail Station see *America Sings* (in the big, round building opposite the Rocket Jets).

22. Exiting *America Sings*, bear left and experience *Captain EO*.

23. Go left upon exiting *Captain EO* and see the *Mission to Mars*.

24. Next ride the PeopleMover which is accessible via escalator at the base of the Rocket Jets platform.

25. Moving toward the main entrance of Tomorrowland, see the film at the Circle-Vision Theater.

26. Depart Tomorrowland and walk to Main Street via the central hub. On your way up Main Street stop for a few minutes at the Main Street Cinema.

27. At the Railroad Station end of Main Street turn left and see *The Walt Disney Story* featuring *Great Moments with Mr. Lincoln*.

28. Next take the Disneyland Railroad for a lap of the park, staying on board for $\frac{1}{4}$ of a second circuit and finally disembarking at the New Orleans Square Station.

29. Turn left after exiting the Station and proceed to Bear Country. See the *Country Bear Jamboree*.

30. Stop for a break at the Hungry Bear Restaurant if the park is open past 7 P.M.

31. Exit Bear Country, passing New Orleans Square en route to Adventureland. Tour the Swiss Family Treehouse.

32. Turn right upon exiting the Treehouse and proceed to the Enchanted Tiki Room for a show.

33. End of One-Day Touring Plan. If you have some time and energy left, enjoy any parades or live entertainment scheduled. If there are any rides you missed earlier, the lines just before closing will be vastly diminished. And remember, Main Street stays open a half hour to an hour later than the rest of Disneyland.

What You Missed

In one day, particularly if the park closes early, it is almost impossible to see and do everything. In the Disneyland One-Day Touring Plan for Adults above, we have bypassed certain rides and other features which, in our opinion, are expendable if you are on a tight (one-day) schedule. If, however, you are curious about what you would be missing, here's a list:

Main Street U.S.A.:	Main Street Buses, Horseless Carriage, etc.
Adventureland:	Nothing missed
New Orleans Square:	Nothing missed
Bear Country:	Davy Crockett's Explorer Canoes
Frontierland:	*Golden Horseshoe Revue* Tom Sawyer Island Mike Fink's Keelboats Big Thunder Ranch
Fantasyland:	Sleeping Beauty Castle Mad Tea Party Dumbo the Flying Elephant

Fantasyland Autopia
Motor Boat Cruise
Casey Jr. Circus Train or Canal Boats
Skyway to Tomorrowland
King Arthur Carousel

Tomorrowland:

Tomorrowland Autopia
Rocket Jets

Other:

Live shows and parades, etc., for which no reservations are required. These are all worthwhile. Pick up a schedule of shows and activities at City Hall when you enter the park; you may choose to substitute a parade or show for a feature listed on the Touring Plan.

For additional information about rides, shows, and features both included and excluded from this One-Day Touring Plan, see "Disneyland in Detail," pages 47–97.

— Outline of One-Day Touring Plan, for Parents with Young Children —

FOR: **Parents with children too young to tour on their own, without parental supervision (eight years and younger).**

ASSUMES: Periodic stops for rest, restrooms, and refreshment.

TRADE-OFFS: This Touring Plan represents a compromise between the observed tastes of adults and the observed tastes of younger children. Included in this Touring Plan are many of the midway-type rides which your children may have the opportunity to experience (although in less exotic surroundings) at local fairs and amusement parks. These rides in Disneyland often require long waits in line and consume valuable touring time which could be better spent experiencing the many rides and shows which can be found only at a Disney theme park, and which best demonstrate the Disney creative genius. This Touring Plan is heavily weighted toward the tastes of younger children. If you want to balance it a bit, try working out a compromise with your kids to forgo some of the carnival-type rides (Mad Tea Party, Dumbo, King Arthur's Carousel) or rides such as the Motor Boat Cruise or the Autopias.

GENERAL DIRECTIONS: On days of moderate to heavy attendance follow the Touring Plan exactly, deviating only when you do not wish to experience an attraction or ride called for on the Touring Plan. For instance, the Touring Plan may indicate that you go next to Tomorrowland and ride Space Mountain, a roller coaster ride. If you do not enjoy roller coasters, simply skip this step of the plan and proceed to the next step.

Be forewarned that this plan requires a lot of walking and some backtracking; this is necessary to avoid long waits in line. A little extra walking will save you from two to three hours of standing in line. Note also that you may not complete the tour. How far you get will depend on how quickly you move from ride to ride, how many times you pause for rest or food, how quickly and how full the park fills, and what time the park closes.

SHORT-DAY TOURING: Sometimes Disneyland opens at 10 A.M. and closes at either 6 or 7 P.M. As a rule, lighter attendance on these days will compensate for the shortened visiting hours, and the Touring Plan will provide for efficient touring and short waits in line. If you are unlucky enough to encounter big crowds on a short-hours day, you may run out of time before you complete the Touring Plan. If you find Disneyland packed on a day when the park closes early, follow the Touring Plan until the Plan calls for lunch. Then stop and scan the remainder of the Plan and scratch any rides or attractions which are of little or marginal interest to you. After lunch (or a snack if you don't wish to stop for lunch), follow the Touring Plan, but bypass the rides and shows that you crossed off. If you end up with some extra time before closing, hit one or two of the rides you eliminated earlier. If you are visiting Disneyland for the first time and are not sure which rides and shows should be on your "must see" list, see the section of this guide titled "Disneyland in Detail."

LONG LINES: Do not be alarmed if some of the lines seem long when you arrive as instructed by the Touring Plan at a particular ride. The Plan is designed to minimize your waits, and even if a line appears long, trust us that it will move quickly. Over an entire day your waits will average about four to seven minutes per ride, but for two or three rides you may have to wait fifteen or twenty minutes (this will probably occur during the hour before lunch).

This Touring Plan is presented in outline form only. For elaboration of the rationale of the Tour sequencing see the EXPLANATION column of the One-Day Touring Plan, for Adults, above.

1. Call (714) 999-4565 the night before your visit to determine the "official" opening time.

2. Arrive at least one hour before the park opens. Buy your admission and enter the park.

3. Proceed directly to the end of Main Street and wait to be admitted to the rest of the park.

4. If your children are of elementary school age and are plucky, go to Tomorrowland and ride Star Tours, a fairly wild space flight simulation ride. If your children are younger, or easily frightened, proceed to Step 6.

5. Exit right and ride Space Mountain

6. Cross the park to Adventureland. Ride the Jungle Cruise. If you and your children are big on roller coasters, after the Jungle Cruise,

go to Frontierland and ride Big Thunder Mountain Railroad. If you feel you can pass up Big Thunder, go directly to Step 7.

7. Go via the central hub to Fantasyland: ride Peter Pan's Flight.

8. Step next door and ride Mr. Toad's Wild Ride.

9. Step around the corner to your right and ride Alice in Wonderland.

10. Upon exiting Alice, ride the Mad Tea Party.

11. Walk away from the Mad Tea Party, keeping Matterhorn Mountain on your right. Ride the Motor Boat Cruise.

12. Walk next door and ride the Fantasyland Autopia.

13. Backtrack to the center of Fantasyland. Ride either the Storybook Land Canal Boats or Casey Jr. Circus Train (both cover the same territory).

14. Ride Dumbo the Flying Elephant.

15. Ride King Arthur's Carousel.

16. Ride Pinocchio's Daring Journey.

17. Ride Snow White's Scary Adventures (see Disney, Small Kids, and Scary Stuff, page 38).

18. Return to Adventureland through the central hub, and from there go to New Orleans Square. Ride Pirates of the Caribbean (see Disney, Small Kids, and Scary Stuff, page 38).

19. Go next door and experience the Haunted Mansion (see Disney, Small Kids, and Scary Stuff, page 38).

20. Go to Bear Country. Grab something to eat at the Mile Long Bar or the Hungry Bear Restaurant. If it's early, eat anyway—the food lines will be shorter. If you feel like you can get by snacking from time to time during the day instead of eating lunch, or if the lunch lines are prohibitive when you arrive, defer eating until you reach Tom Sawyer Island.

21. After lunch, while in Bear Country, see the *Country Bear Jamboree*.

22. Take a raft to Tom Sawyer Island, find a shady spot to sit while the kids explore the island. Pick a time and a meeting place to join

back up. If you missed lunch earlier grab a snack at the Fort Wilderness Snack Bar. As concerns Tom Sawyer Island, be advised that (1) your kids would spend a week here if they could, and (2) if you decide to invest a lot of time here (40 minutes or more), you will probably not make it beyond Step 27 or 28 if the park closes at 6 or 7 P.M.

23. Return via raft from the island and proceed to Frontierland. Cruise the Rivers of America on either the Steamboat or the Sailing Ship.

24. Exit Frontierland via the central hub and proceed to Tomorrowland.

25. Walk across the concourse and see the film showing at the CircleVision Theater.

26. Ride the PeopleMover (entrance under the Rocket Jets platform).

27. See *Captain EO* near Space Mountain.

28. Go next door and take in the *Mission to Mars*.

29. Proceed next door and see *America Sings*.

30. Cross the concourse toward Matterhorn Mountain. Ride the Monorail (take a complete round trip; do not exit at the hotel).

31. Passing Matterhorn Mountain on your left, return to Fantasyland and ride It's a Small World.

32. Leave Fantasyland, transiting the central hub, and walk to the Main Street Train Station. Take the Disneyland Railroad all the way around the park, and then, instead of getting off at Main Street, continue to New Orleans Square and disembark.

33. Turn right and proceed to Adventureland. Walk through the Swiss Family Treehouse.

34. Go right upon exiting the Treehouse and walk to the Enchanted Tiki Room. See the show.

35. This is the end of the Touring Plan. If you have any time left before closing (or any energy, for that matter) try some of the evening parades and live entertainment offerings. Rides that you missed earlier for whatever reason will have vastly diminished lines in the hour before closing if you wish to try again. The Submarine

Voyage in Tomorrowland (not included in the Touring Plan) is a good bet for this time of day. And remember, Main Street will remain open a half hour to an hour after everything else closes.

What You Missed

Listed below is a summary of the rides, shows, and attractions you will not see on this One-Day Touring Plan:

On Main Street:	*Walt Disney Story/Great Moments with Mr. Lincoln* Main Street Cinema Main Street Buses, Horseless Carriage, Fire Engines
In Adventureland:	Nothing missed
In New Orleans Square:	Nothing missed
In Bear Country:	Davy Crockett's Explorer Canoes
In Frontierland:	*Golden Horseshoe Revue* Mike Fink Keelboats Big Thunder Ranch
In Fantasyland:	Sleeping Beauty Castle Casey Jr. Circus Train or Canal Boats
In Tomorrowland:	Rocket Jets Tomorrowland Autopia Submarine Voyage

—— Outline of One-Day Touring Plan, for Parents with Older Children ——

FOR: **For parents with children old enough to tour partly or entirely on their own.**

ASSUMES: Children 9 years of age or older touring without direct supervision but meeting their parents periodically throughout the day.

GENERAL DIRECTIONS: On days of moderate to heavy attendance follow the Touring Plan exactly, deviating only when you do not wish to experience an attraction or ride called for on the Touring Plan. For instance, the Touring Plan may indicate that you go next to Tomorrowland and ride Space Mountain, a roller coaster ride. If you do not enjoy roller coasters, simply skip this step of the plan and proceed to the next step.

Be forewarned that this plan requires a lot of walking and some backtracking; this is necessary to avoid long waits in line. A little extra walking will save you from two to three hours of standing in line. Note also that you may not complete the tour. How far you get will depend on how quickly you move from ride to ride, how many times you pause for rest or food, how quickly and how full the park fills, and what time the park closes.

SHORT-DAY TOURING: Sometimes Disneyland opens at 10 A.M. and closes at either 6 or 7 P.M. As a rule, lighter attendance on these days will compensate for the shortened visiting hours and the Touring Plan will provide for efficient touring and short waits in line. If you are unlucky enough to encounter big crowds on a short-hours day, you may run out of time before you complete the Touring Plan. If you find Disneyland packed on a day when the park closes early, follow the Touring Plan until the Plan calls for lunch. Then stop and scan the remainder of the Plan and scratch any rides or attractions which are of little or marginal interest to you. After lunch (or a snack if you don't wish to stop for lunch), follow the Touring Plan, but bypass the rides and shows that you crossed off. If you end up with some extra time before closing, hit one or two of the rides you eliminated earlier. If you are visiting Disneyland for the first time and are not sure which rides and shows should be on your "must see" list, see the section of this guide titled "Disneyland in Detail."

LONG LINES: Do not be alarmed if some of the lines seem long when you arrive, as instructed by the Touring Plan, at a particular ride. The Plan is designed to minimize your waits, and even if a line appears long, trust us that it will move quickly. Over an entire day your waits will average about four to seven minutes per ride, but for two or three rides you may have to wait fifteen or twenty minutes (this will probably occur during the hour before lunch).

This Touring Plan is presented in outline form only. For elaboration of the rationale of the Tour sequencing see the EXPLANATION column of the One-Day Touring Plan, for Adults, above.

PARENT DIRECTION	YOUNG PERSON'S DIRECTION
1. On the day before you tour, call (714) 999-4565 to determine the official opening time of the park.	**1.** Bone up on all the things you want to see.
2. Arrive at the park one hour before the official opening time. Eat breakfast before you go.	**2.** Same as parents' Step 2.
3. Buy your admission and make a note of any rides or attractions that are closed (posted on every ticket booth). Enter the park and wait at the end of Main Street for the rest of Disneyland to open.	**3.** Same as parents' Step 3.
4. When the rest of the park opens, go directly to Tomorrowland and ride Star Tours.	**4.** Go to Tomorrowland and ride Star Tours.
5. Exit right and ride Space Mountain. If you don't enjoy roller coasters, go to Step 6.	**5.** Exit right and ride Space Mountain. If you don't like roller coasters, go directly across Tomorrowland and ride the Submarine Voyage.
6. Walk across Tomorrowland and ride the Submarine Voyage.	**6.** Go through Tomorrowland and into Fantasyland. Ride the

PARENT DIRECTION	YOUNG PERSON'S DIRECTION
	Matterhorn Bobsleds. If you don't like roller coasters, go to Step 7.
7. Go to Fantasyland, passing the Matterhorn on your left, and ride Alice in Wonderland.	**7.** Go to Fantasyland; ride the Mad Tea Party.
8. Go around the corner to your left upon exiting Alice; ride Mr. Toad's Wild Ride.	**8.** Ride Alice in Wonderland.
9. Go next door and ride Peter Pan's Flight.	**9.** Ride Mr. Toad's Wild Ride.
10. Walk across the street and ride Snow White's Scary Adventures.	**10.** Ride Peter Pan's Flight.
11. Go next door and ride Pinocchio's Daring Journey.	**11.** Ride Snow White's Scary Adventures.
12. Go to Adventureland via the central hub; ride the Jungle Cruise.	**12.** Ride Pinocchio's Daring Journey.
13. Go to New Orleans Square and ride Pirates of the Caribbean.	**13.** Go to Adventureland and ride the Jungle Cruise.
14. Visit the Haunted Mansion.	**14.** Go to New Orleans Square and ride Pirates of the Caribbean.
15. Proceed to Frontierland and ride Big Thunder Mountain Railroad. This is more of a Disney Adventure than a thrill ride. Even if you passed up earlier roller coaster offerings, we think you will like Big Thunder Mountain.	**15.** Visit the Haunted Mansion.
16. Go to the Casa Mexicana restaurant across from the en-	**16.** Go to Frontierland and ride Big Thunder Mountain Railroad.

PARENT DIRECTION	YOUNG PERSON'S DIRECTION
trance of Big Thunder Mountain. Grab a table and get in line for lunch; the young folks will be along in a few minutes.	After riding, meet your elders at the Casa Mexicana Restaurant across from the entrance of Big Thunder.
17. After lunch, but before leaving the restaurant, make arrangements to meet the young folks at the Tomorrowland Terrace (another restaurant) at 3:30 P.M. Whoever gets there first grabs a table and waits for the others.	**17.** Before leaving make arrangements to meet at the Tomorrowland Terrace Restaurant at 3:30 P.M. Whoever gets there first grabs a table and waits for the others.
18. After lunch walk to the Steamboat landing and take either the Mark Twain or the Columbia for a cruise on the Rivers of America. You will be able to see the boats docking from the restaurant, so just wait until one pulls in and unloads before you walk over to board.	**18.** Take a cruise on the Columbia Sailing Ship or on the Mark Twain Steamboat. Or, if you don't mind a little waiting in line, walk around the landing to Bear Country and ride instead the Davy Crockett's Explorer Canoes (more fun than the larger boats). Watch during lunch to see if any canoes go by. On some days the canoes do not operate.
19. Next, return to Fantasyland and ride Casey Jr. Circus Train or the Storybook Land Canal Boats. Since they both cover the same scenery, pick the one that has the shortest line (usually Casey Jr.).	**19.** After whichever river cruise you take, go to the *Country Bear Jamboree* in Bear Country.
20. Keeping the Matterhorn to your right, walk through Fantasyland to It's a Small World. Enjoy the ride.	**20.** Take a raft to Tom Sawyer Island and have a ball. If the park closes early and you only have one day at Disneyland, don't stay too long.
21. Return to Tomorrowland walking with the Matterhorn on	**21.** Go to the New Orleans Square Train Station and catch

PARENT DIRECTION	YOUNG PERSON'S DIRECTION
your right. At the edge of the Submarine lagoon catch the Monorail for a round trip.	the Disneyland Railroad. Ride ¾ of a complete circuit and get off at Main Street Station.
22. Walk across Tomorrowland and see *America Sings*.	**22.** Return to Tomorrowland.
NOTE: Don't forget to meet your group at Tomorrowland Terrace at 3:30 P.M. During this meeting designate a time and a place for a later meeting, and determine plans for the evening meal.	NOTE: Don't forget to meet your group at Tomorrowland Terrace at 3:30 P.M.
23. Go next door to experience the *Mission to Mars*.	**23.** See *Captain EO* at the base of Space Mountain.
24. Ride the PeopleMover (loads beneath the Rocket Jets platform).	**24.** Experience the *Mission to Mars*.
25. View *Captain EO* at the base of Space Mountain.	**25.** See *America Sings*.
26. See the film at the Circle-Vision Theater.	**26.** See the film at the Circle-Vision Theater.
27. Exit Tomorrowland via its main entrance and walk to the Railroad Station end of Main Street. See *The Walt Disney Story* featuring *Great Moments with Mr. Lincoln*.	**27.** Go to the Tomorrowland Monorail Station; take the Monorail for a round trip ride.
28. Board the Disneyland Railroad at the Main Street Station. Make a complete circuit of the park and then stay on board for ¼ of a second circuit, finally disembarking at New Orleans Square.	**28.** Go to Fantasyland with the Matterhorn on your left. Ride It's a Small World.

PARENT DIRECTION	YOUNG PERSON'S DIRECTION
29. Turn left out of the New Orleans Square Station and head for Bear Country. See the *Country Bear Jamboree*.	**29.** Exit Fantasyland, and cross the central hub to Adventureland. Walk through the Swiss Family Treehouse.
30. Return to Adventureland. Walk through the Swiss Family Treehouse.	**30.** Take in a performance at the Enchanted Tiki Room.
31. Exit to the right from the Treehouse and walk over to the Enchanted Tiki Room for a performance.	**31.** If the park is open late and you still have some time and energy, try the Videopolis, Disneyland's teen nightclub located to the left of It's a Small World (in Fantasyland).
32. This completes the Touring Plan. If you have time and/or energy remaining, enjoy the live evening entertainment, revisit your favorite attractions, or return to any rides or shows that were not operating earlier.	**32.** This completes the Touring Plan. If you have any time left, indulge yourself according to your interests. Note that lines for rides will be much shorter the hour before closing.

What You Missed

In one day, particularly if the park closes early, it is almost impossible to see and do everything. In the Disneyland One-Day Touring Plan 3 above, we have bypassed certain rides and other features which, in our opinion, are expendable if you are on a tight (one-day) schedule. If, however, you are curious about what you would be missing, here's a list:

Main Street U.S.A.:	Main Street Buses, Horseless Carriage, etc. *Walt Disney Story* (younger folks)
Adventureland:	Nothing missed
New Orleans Square:	Nothing missed
Bear Country:	Davy Crockett's Explorer Canoes (older folks)

Frontierland:	*Golden Horseshoe Revue* Tom Sawyer Island (older folks) Mike Fink's Keelboats
Fantasyland:	Sleeping Beauty Castle Mad Tea Party (older folks) Dumbo the Flying Elephant Fantasyland Autopia Motor Boat Cruise Casey Jr. Circus Train or Canal Boats Skyway to Tomorrowland King Arthur Carousel Matterhorn Bobsleds (older folks)
Tomorrowland:	Tomorrowland Autopia Rocket Jets
Other:	Live shows and parades, etc., for which no reservations are required. These are all worthwhile. Pick up a schedule of shows and activities at City Hall when you enter the park; you may choose to substitute a parade or show for a feature listed on the Touring Plan.

—— Outline of One-Day Touring Plan, for Mature Visitors ——

FOR: **Mature visitors who wish to see as much as possible in one day while minimizing the amount of walking necessary.**

ASSUMES: Stops for rest, food, and refreshment. Also assumes a willingness to experience new things.

NOTE: Minimizing walking and seeing most of Disneyland in one day is a contradiction in terms on a busy day. For this reason, the Touring Plan for Mature Visitors tends to be more selective in terms of rides, shows, and attractions visited. Thus, using this Touring Plan, you will see those features which are preeminent at Disneyland plus those less acclaimed features which are proven favorites of the more mature audience. Another feature of this Touring Plan is the frequent use of the various in-park transportation facilities (instead of walking) to travel from one area to another. Further detail on individual rides, shows, and features can be found in the "Disneyland in Detail" section beginning on page 45.

Many mature visitors walk routinely for exercise. If you and the members of your group are used to taking long walks, you might prefer the One-Day Touring Plan for Adults which will require more hiking but will allow you to see more of the park in a single day.

GENERAL DIRECTIONS: On days of moderate to heavy attendance follow the Touring Plan exactly, deviating only when you do not wish to experience an attraction or ride called for on the Touring Plan. For instance, the Touring Plan may indicate that you go next to Tomorrowland and ride the Skyway, a cable car ride. If you are apprehensive about heights, simply skip this step of the plan and proceed to the next step.

Be forewarned that this plan requires a lot of walking and some backtracking; this is necessary to avoid long waits in line. A little extra walking will save you from two to three hours of standing in line. Note also that you may not complete the tour. How far you get will depend on how quickly you move from ride to ride, how many times you pause for rest or food, how quickly and how full the park fills, and what time the park closes.

SHORT-DAY TOURING: Sometimes Disneyland opens at 10 A.M. and closes at either 6 or 7 P.M. As a rule, lighter attendance on these days will compensate for the shortened visiting hours and the Touring Plan will provide for efficient touring and short waits in line. If you are unlucky enough to encounter big crowds on a short-hours day, you may run out of time before you complete the Touring Plan. If you find Disneyland packed on a day when the park closes early, follow the Touring Plan until the Plan calls for lunch. Then stop and scan the remainder of the Plan and scratch any rides or attractions which are of little or marginal interest to you. After lunch (or a snack if you don't wish to stop for lunch), follow the Touring Plan, but bypass the rides and shows that you crossed off. If you end up with some extra time before closing, try one or two of the rides you eliminated earlier. If you are visiting Disneyland for the first time and are not sure which rides and shows should be on your "must see" list, see the section of this guide titled "Disneyland in Detail."

LONG LINES: Do not be alarmed if some of the lines seem long when you arrive as per the Touring Plan at a particular ride. The Plan is designed to minimize your waits, and even if a line appears long, trust us that it will move quickly. Over an entire day your waits will average about four to seven minutes per ride, but for two or three rides you may have to wait fifteen or twenty minutes (this will probably occur during the hour before lunch).

This Touring Plan is presented in outline form only. For elaboration of the rationale of the Tour sequencing see the EXPLANATION column of the One-Day Touring Plan for Adults, above.

1. Call (714) 999-4565 the night before your visit to determine the "official" opening time.

2. Arrive at least one hour before the park opens. Buy your admission and enter the park.

3. Proceed directly to the end of Main Street and wait to be admitted to the rest of the park.

4. When you are admitted to the rest of the park, go directly to Adventureland and ride the Jungle Cruise.

5. Exit Adventureland the way you entered and proceed via the central hub to Fantasyland, passing through the entrance to the Castle. Ride Peter Pan's Flight.

6. Walk next door and ride Mr. Toad's Wild Ride.

7. Turn right upon exiting Mr. Toad and go right again at the corner to ride Alice in Wonderland (do not confuse with the Mad Tea Party, a carnival-type ride).

8. Keeping the Matterhorn on your right and the Canal Boats on your left, walk to the rear of Fantasyland and ride It's a Small World.

9. Retracing your steps, walk back toward the Castle. Circle around the Carousel to the left and ride Snow White's Scary Adventures.

10. Moving away from the Castle, go next door and ride Pinocchio's Daring Journey.

11. Turn left upon exiting Pinocchio and proceed to the Skyway. Ride the Skyway to Tomorrowland.

12. Turn to your right after exiting the Skyway and proceed to the Tomorrowland Railroad Station. Catch the Disneyland Railroad and ride to New Orleans Square (second stop after you board).

13. After disembarking at New Orleans Square, bear right. Ride Pirates of the Caribbean.

14. Go left after exiting Pirates of the Caribbean and walk to the Haunted Mansion. Ride.

15. Proceed to the waterfront and ride the keel boats. Try to get a seat on top.

16. With the waterfront on your right, walk to Bear Country. We recommend that you take the Monorail to the Disneyland Hotel complex for a nice relaxing, sit-down lunch away from the crowds (see Step 20). If, however, you prefer to eat in the park, eat now at the Hungry Bear Restaurant next to *Country Bear Jamboree*.

17. See the *Country Bear Jamboree*.

18. Return to the New Orleans Square Railroad Station and catch a train back to Tomorrowland.

19. Disembarking at Tomorrowland, proceed to the Tomorrowland Monorail Station (over by the Submarines) and take the Monorail to the Disneyland Hotel complex for lunch. Be sure to have your hand stamped for reentry to the park when you get off at the hotel.

If you have already eaten, do not disembark at the hotel. Continue aboard for a round trip back to Tomorrowland.

20. After lunch, return to the park via the Monorail.

21. Returning to Tomorrowland, see *America Sings* (large round building).

22. Proceed next door to the left and experience *Captain EO.*

23. Board the PeopleMover via the escalator under the Rocket Jets platform.

24. After riding the PeopleMover, see the film featured at the Circle-Vision Theater.

25. Now ride Star Tours opposite the Circle-Vision Theater.

26. Depart Tomorrowland and proceed via the central hub to Adventureland. Take in a performance at the Enchanted Tiki Room.

27. Exit Adventureland and go to Main Street. Walk to the Railroad Station end of Main Street and bear left for a performance of the *Walt Disney Story* featuring *Great Moments with Mr. Lincoln.*

28. End of this Touring Plan. If you have some time remaining before the park closes, take in some of the live entertainment offerings, or catch some of the rides or attractions you may have missed earlier. The lines for all rides are vastly diminished during the hour before closing. Remember, Main Street closes a half hour to an hour later than the rest of the park. If you stay for some additional touring, bear in mind that you can reach New Orleans Square or Tomorrowland via the Disneyland Railroad.

What You Missed

In one day, particularly if the park closes early, it is almost impossible to see and do everything. In the One-Day Touring Plan for Mature Visitors above, we have bypassed certain rides and other features which, in our opinion, are expendable if you are on a tight (one-day) schedule. If, however, you are curious about what you would be missing, here's a list:

Main Street U.S.A.:	Main Street Buses, Horseless Carriage, etc.
Adventureland:	Swiss Family Treehouse

New Orleans Square: Nothing missed

Bear Country: Davy Crockett's Explorer Canoes

Frontierland: *Golden Horseshoe Revue*
Tom Sawyer Island
Mark Twain Steamboat/Sailing Ship Columbia
Big Thunder Mountain Railroad

Fantasyland: Sleeping Beauty Castle
Mad Tea Party
Dumbo the Flying Elephant
Fantasyland Autopia
Motor Boat Cruise
Casey Jr. Circus Train or Canal Boats
King Arthur Carousel
Matterhorn Bobsleds

Tomorrowland: Tomorrowland Autopia
Rocket Jets
Space Mountain
Submarine Voyage

Other: Live shows and parades, etc., for which no reservations are required. These are all worthwhile. Pick up a schedule of shows and activities at City Hall when you enter the park; you may choose to substitute a parade or show for a feature listed on the Touring Plan.

— Outline of Two-Day Touring Plan —

FOR: **Visitors who have two or more days to visit Disneyland.**

GENERAL: The Two-Day Touring Plan provides an itinerary for two days of touring. The Plan allows time to experience almost all rides and attractions without rush and with plenty of time left for enjoying the park's live entertainment offerings and for shopping. Options incorporated into the Touring Plan make it useful to all categories of visitors.

DIRECTIONS: On days of moderate to heavy attendance follow the Touring Plan exactly, deviating only when you do not wish to experience an attraction or a ride called for on the Touring Plan. For instance, the Touring Plan may indicate that you go next to Tomorrowland and ride the Skyway, a cable car ride. If you are apprehensive about heights, simply skip this step of the plan and proceed to the next step.

Day One

1. Call (714) 999-4565 the night before your visit to determine the "official" opening time.

2. Arrive at least one hour before the park opens. Buy your admission and enter the park.

3. Proceed directly to the end of Main Street and wait to be admitted to the rest of the park.

4. When you are admitted to the rest of the park, go directly to Tomorrowland and ride Star Tours.

5. Exit right and ride Space Mountain.

6. Walk across Tomorrowland to Fantasyland and ride the Matterhorn Bobsleds.

7. Backtrack slightly to Tomorrowland and ride the Submarine Voyage.

8. Proceed to Fantasyland and ride Alice in Wonderland.

9. Walking around the corner toward the Castle, ride Mr. Toad's Wild Ride.

10. Go next door and ride Peter Pan's Flight.

11. Go across the walkway and ride Snow White's Scary Adventures.

12. Walking away from the Castle, go next door and ride Pinocchio's Daring Journey.

13. Proceed to the far side of the Carousel and ride the Storybook Land Canal Boats.

    If you have small children in your group, now is the time for them to ride Dumbo the Flying Elephant, King Arthur's Carousel, and the Mad Tea Party, in that order. Parties with small children should then ride the Fantasyland Autopia and the Motor Boat Cruise before continuing to Step 14.

14. Go next to the rear of Fantasyland and ride It's a Small World.

15. Return to Tomorrowland and see *America Sings*.

16. Experience the *Mission to Mars*.

17. Take the Monorail to the Disneyland Hotel complex for lunch. Have your hand stamped for reentry to the park when you disembark at the hotel.

18. Return to the park via the Monorail. Since there will be plenty of time to complete the remainder of the first day's Touring Plan, feel free to attend the afternoon parade or enjoy any of the other live entertainment offerings during the afternoon and evening. Return to the Touring Plan when it suits your wishes.

19. In Tomorrowland see *Captain EO* in the theater at the base of Space Mountain.

20. Ride the PeopleMover, loading via the escalator at the base of the Rocket Jets platform.

21. In Tomorrowland see the film featured at the Circle-Vision Theater.

22. This completes the Touring Plan for Day One. If the park is open past 7:00 you may wish to go to your hotel for a rest and dinner,

returning to enjoy Disneyland at night. If the park closes early, use your remaining time to enjoy some live entertainment, to people watch, to shop, or to do whatever moves you.

Day Two

1. Call (714) 999-4565 the night before your visit to determine the "official" opening time.

2. Arrive at least one hour before the park opens. Buy your admission and enter the park.

3. Proceed directly to the end of Main Street and wait to be admitted to the rest of the park.

4. Go to Frontierland and ride Big Thunder Mountain Railroad (sometimes immediately after opening you are given the option to ride a second time before exiting). If there is someone in your party who doesn't care for roller coasters, have them proceed to Step 5. Meet them at the Golden Horseshoe after your ride.

5. Go to the Golden Horseshoe in Frontierland and make reservations for your party for the 1 P.M. showing of the *Golden Horseshoe Revue* (they start taking reservations 15 minutes after Frontierland opens).

6. Head back toward the entrance of Frontierland. At the end of the boardwalk turn right for a shortcut to Adventureland. Ride the Jungle Cruise.

7. Turn left to New Orleans Square after exiting the Jungle Cruise. Ride Pirates of the Caribbean.

8. Turn left after exiting Pirates of the Caribbean and experience the Haunted Mansion.

9. Continue left after leaving the Haunted Mansion and enter Bear Country. Ride Davy Crockett's Explorer Canoes.

10. Go next in Bear Country to the *Country Bear Jamboree*.

11. Leave Bear Country and walk to the landing in front of the Haunted Mansion. Take a raft to Tom Sawyer Island. Explore the island until about noon. At noon take a raft back across the river.

12. Go to the Golden Horseshoe in Frontierland and wait to be seated for the *Golden Horseshoe Revue*.

13. At the Golden Horseshoe, eat lunch and see the show.

14. For a different view of the Rivers of America, take a cruise on the Mark Twain Steamboat or on the Sailing Ship Columbia.

15. Return to New Orleans Square and take the Disneyland Railroad to Main Street.

16. You should arrive approximately in time for the afternoon parade; the best vantage point is the platform level of the Main Street Train Station. If you have more than 30 minutes before the parade begins, go to Step 17 and then return to watch the parade. If you have less than 30 minutes, find a nice viewing spot on the platform and take a break.

17. See *The Walt Disney Story* featuring *Great Moments with Mr. Lincoln*, located to the immediate right of the Main Street Train Station as you look toward the central hub.

18. Spend a little time in the Main Street Cinema, on the right-hand side of the street as you walk toward the central hub.

19. Return to Adventureland. Tour the Swiss Family Treehouse.

20. Turn right upon exiting the Treehouse. See the show at the Enchanted Tiki Room (if this attraction has a long line, return later at your convenience).

21. Enjoy the shops, live entertainment, and other offerings of Disneyland.

22. Tour Sleeping Beauty's Castle in Fantasyland (enter to your immediate left as you emerge from the Castle entrance into the Fantasyland square).

23. While in Fantasyland ride the Skyway to Tomorrowland.

24. This completes the Touring Plan for Day Two. If the park is open past 7 P.M. you may wish to go to your hotel for a rest and dinner, returning to enjoy Disneyland at night. If the park closes early, use your remaining time to enjoy some live entertainment, to people watch, to shop, or to do whatever moves you.

— *Not to Be Missed at Disneyland* —

Adventureland	Jungle Cruise
Bear Country	*Country Bear Jamboree*
Fantasyland	It's a Small World
	Peter Pan's Flight
New Orleans Square	Haunted Mansion
	Pirates of the Caribbean
Tomorrowland	*America Sings*
	Space Mountain
	Submarine Voyage
	World Premier Circle-Vision
	Captain EO
	Star Tours

Index